HOW TO COLLEGE

How to COLLEGE

WHAT TO KNOW BEFORE YOU GO
(AND WHEN YOU'RE THERE)

Andrea Malkin Brenner
AND Lara Hope Schwartz

ST. MARTIN'S GRIFFIN
NEW YORK

HOW TO COLLEGE. Copyright © 2019 by Andrea Malkin Brenner and Lara Hope Schwartz. All rights reserved. Printed in the United States of America. For information, address St. Martin's Press, 175 Fifth Avenue, New York, N.Y. 10010.

www.stmartins.com

Book design by Richard Oriolo

Library of Congress Cataloging-in-Publication Data

Names: Brenner, Andrea (Andrea Malkin), author. | Schwartz, Lara (Lara Hope), author.
Title: How to college : what to know before you go (and when you're there) / Andrea Malkin Brenner and Lara Hope Schwartz.
Description: First edition. | New York : St. Martin's Griffin, 2019. | Includes bibliographical references and index.
Identifiers: LCCN 2019000551| ISBN 9781250225184 (trade pbk.) | ISBN 9781250225191 (ebook)
Subjects: LCSH: College student orientation—United States—Handbooks, manuals, etc. | College freshmen—United States—Life skills guides. | College students—United States—Conduct of life—Handbooks, manuals, etc. | Education, Higher—United States—Handbooks, manuals, etc.
Classification: LCC LB2343.32 .B7 2019 | DDC 378.1/98—dc23
LC record available at https://lccn.loc.gov/2019000551

Our books may be purchased in bulk for promotional, educational, or business use. Please contact your local bookseller or the Macmillan Corporate and Premium Sales Department at 1-800-221-7945, extension 5442, or by email at MacmillanSpecialMarkets@macmillan.com.

First Edition: April 2019

10   9

To our students

And in memory of Carol Fine Malkin and Adele Zweig
Schwartz who taught us what matters

CONTENTS

PART III: TAKE CARE OF YOU

PART IV: THE RESIDENT EXPERTS

PART V: MONEY TALK

PART VI: LIFE BEYOND THE CLASSROOM

PART VII: YOUR TO-DO LIST

AN INTRODUCTION FOR STUDENTS

You've put in a lot of thought and hard work to get where you are now: an "almost" college student. But if you're like the thousands of students we've worked with over the years, you've got questions, concerns, and anxieties about what's to come. And that makes sense—the transition from high school—and home—to college can be stressful for you and your family. That's true whether you're the first person in your family to go to college or not.

College is wonderful—but it's different from high school. College is challenging—and it's supposed to be. It's the *transition* to college that's often the most stressful part for incoming students and their families.

Here's the good news:

1. **WHAT IT TAKES** to succeed in college is mysterious, but it isn't rocket science (our apologies to aerospace engineering majors). When you understand what it's all about, you're going to feel a lot better.

2. **PREPARATION HELPS.** You already know this from your experience with tests, sports, or performances.

This book will take the mystery out of what college is all about ("adulting") and recommend simple, important, and practical steps you should take to set yourself up for success. *How to College* covers the whole campus experience: living and learning with peers; college-level academics; taking care of yourself; finding and using resources; handling your finances; and getting around (and involved) on and off campus.

In addition to insiders' advice about adulting that really works, *How to College* includes four types of activities:

- **KNOW BEFORE YOU GO:** In these exercises, you'll be asked to find answers to questions specific to you or your college. For example, you need to understand your health insurance coverage, including how to find a participating provider and what a "copay" is; figure out how to use the public transportation options near your new campus; and know the differences between terms such as *stress* and *distress*.

- **DO BEFORE YOU GO:** These are activities you should complete before move-in day. For example, you should make appointments with your healthcare providers; introduce yourself to your professors with a professional email; and add tools such as a shuttle bus tracker and your college's suggested safety apps to your smartphone.

- **DISCUSS BEFORE YOU GO:** These are topics to discuss with your parent(s) or your family, with conversation prompts to get you started. For example, how often do you expect to communicate with your family, and how? What role will your family play on move-in day? What backup plans do you have for uncomfortable and potentially dangerous situations you might encounter during your first semester? Which expenses (if any) will your family pay directly and which will be your responsibility?

- **WHEN YOU'RE THERE:** These are expert tips about how to succeed and thrive in your first year, including advice for reading, studying, and writing; maintaining your health; getting involved on and off campus; and more. Preparation is essential, but these tips are about how to college once you're *at college,* so make sure to pack this book when you head to school.

After completing the exercises in this book, you should be able to tackle the college transition and its typical challenges—whether it's a roommate conflict, a disappointing grade, or your first illness away from home.

You'll notice that the tone of this guide is both serious and fun. That's what college and adulting are like, too. You'll experience pride in your accomplishments *and* in learning from your mistakes and mishaps. Some things will be difficult, and the stakes are also high; that's something to take seriously. But we want you to know that college should be a joyful time of new experiences, friends, learning, questioning, and freedoms.

You've probably also noticed that we're talking directly to *you,* the (almost) college student. In college, you'll make more decisions yourself. You will be your professors' only point of contact about your academics (learn more about that in chapter 5); you'll be responsible for getting enough sleep and consuming healthy food (chapter 9); and you'll start building your future through internships and jobs (chapter 19). Your family will play a role as you prepare to leave for college (and will be a resource when you're there, too), but this is yours to do.

You'll also be expected to manage your time in college. As your first act of adulting, start now by planning what you should know, do, and discuss before leaving for campus. You'll find a checklist at the end of the book that includes all the exercises we've included throughout the book. Some will be more relevant or interesting to you than others. *You* decide how you'll tackle them. Setting priorities is an adulting skill. Remember—you're in charge. You're (almost) a college student.

WE NEED TO SEE OTHER PEOPLE: A LETTER TO PARENTS AND FAMILIES

Have you ever had a conversation that began, "We need to see other people"? This book is one of those. It is an eye-opening recognition that your student is on the path to adulthood. It's time for them to learn what you've already learned: that in adulthood, we must build a healthy and productive network of support and mentorship that includes people beyond the family.

This book is addressed to your student for a reason: at its core, *How to College* is a subset of "How to Be an Adult." And that means we're speaking to your student as the adult you want them to be, and the adult they will be *expected* to be when college begins. You might have bought this book for your student, and if so, we know you share our belief that there's a lot to learn, and that preparation matters.

In our work with thousands of first-year college students (and as parents ourselves), we've learned that a young person's transition from high school student to college student (and emerging adult) doesn't happen overnight. As parents and families, you play a very important role in supporting your student in taking steps toward independence. That's true whether you went to college yourself or not; this book is written for every student and every family.

What can you do? First, read the book yourself, if you'd like. We recommend that you have a look at the "Know and Do Before You Go" checklist on page 272, which outlines what we recommend students do before they leave for campus. Next, your job is to support and encourage them to use this book—not to take the lead in their preparation for college. That's *their* job. If you see something on the checklist that you feel is particularly important for them to address, let them know.

This book is about adulting, and that includes honest conversations between you and your emerging adult about how to prepare. It should include your concerns and priorities as well. The "Discuss Before You Go" exercises in this book are very important. These include prompts for conversations that current college students have told us they wished they'd had with their parents and families before leaving home. These exercises also include prompts for conversations that parents and families have told us they wish they'd had with their kids before those kids left for college. We encourage you to prepare for these conversations by considering your new rules and expectations. The transition to college from home and high school is a significant one, and we all want it to go as smoothly as possible.

Finally, since your student is taking steps into your adult world, it's only fair that you take a step into their world as a student and do some homework, too:

Perspective Taking

Picture your younger self moving away from home for the first time.

- What were you most worried about?
- What excited you the most?
- What do you wish your parent(s) or family had understood about that transition for you?
- What did they do well?
- What do you wish they'd done differently?

Look at your younger self from your current perspective as an adult.

- What do you wish you had known (that a family member could have told you)?
- What did you get wrong?
- What would your present-day self say to your younger self?
- How did the real experience measure up to your worry, excitement, and expectations?

Now that your student's transition away from home feels closer to you, consider these questions as if *you* were your student:

- I'm worried my parent/supporting family member won't understand _____.
- It's hard for me to talk to them about _____.
- I'm concerned that they will worry about me doing _____.
- Now that I'm going to live on my own, I need more freedom to _____.
- I hope they can support me in doing _____.

A GUIDE TO THIS GUIDE

At the back of this book, you'll find four checklists you can use to plan and keep track of your preparation:

1. **DO THIS. NOW. SERIOUSLY. (PAGE 271):** A list of essential documents you *must* submit to your school this summer.

2. **KNOW AND DO BEFORE YOU GO (PAGE 272):** A checklist of all the tasks and exercises found throughout this book.

3. **MAKE YOUR SMARTPHONE SMARTER (PAGE 277):** A checklist of apps, information, and contact information to install on your phone.

4. **BOOST YOUR BROWSER (PAGE 278):** A list of important websites you should bookmark on your browser.

A NOTE ON PLANNING YOUR WORK WITH THIS BOOK

Most of the exercises found in this book will require little time to complete. A few of them will take a bit longer.

- Two exercises—the time-tracking exercise ("168 Self-Assessment," page 130) and the budget-tracking exercise (page 215)—require you to keep track of your activities and spending, respectively, for one week. We strongly suggest that you complete both exercises over a week when you aren't away on vacation.

- If you have not yet done so, we recommend that you take a free or low-cost self-defense course and a financial literacy workshop. Look into these well in advance so you can budget time for them.

PART I

THE NEW COLLEGE YOU

College is around the corner. Chances are, you've got some mixed emotions about what your new campus environment will feel like. What is this "new college you" that everyone is talking about? Is your identity really going to change when you become a college student? What about meeting your new roommate(s) and the other students in your residence hall—what if you don't find people to connect with? What if you say the wrong thing?

The first section of this book will answer all those questions and hopefully help quell many of your fears by preparing you for common first-year pitfalls. It also offers insider advice from staff, faculty, and students to help you with that transition. We'll discuss the differences between your high school and college identities; how to introduce yourself to others (including on social media); and how to avoid "imposter syndrome."

In exploring what it really means to be independent, you'll learn some tips on communicating with your family and how to responsibly speak your mind as a new college student. We'll dive into building new relationships with your roommate(s), hall mates, and other students on your campus, and openly discuss the nervousness and excitement that comes with stepping out of your comfort zone—perhaps more than you ever have.

1

YOUR IDENTITY: IS REINVENTING
YOURSELF A REAL THING?

Although it is good to have goals, you don't need to figure out your
whole life during your first semester. Set goals, but focus on the short-
term goals of your first semester rather than the long-term goals of
your college career or the rest of your life.

—COLLEGE STUDENT

Y̲ou do *not* need to have your life plan figured out during your
first semester (or even during your first year) of college. You'll
have time to select your major (and even change it, if you want
or need to), finish your academic requirements, and choose at least your
first career path before you graduate.

Your first semester on campus is not the time to worry about how
the next four years will play out. Instead, it is a time to try new things,
like pushing yourself outside your comfort zone, immersing yourself
in challenging academic work, learning to ask intellectual questions,

experiencing new social situations, meeting people whose lived experiences have been different from your own, and taking some (not-too-risky) risks. Your post–high school self will shift and develop as you encounter these new experiences. Shaping and growing your mind, body, and spirit is a gradual process, and there's no reason to rush it.

HIGH SCHOOL YOU VS. COLLEGE YOU

Don't forget that when you began high school, there was always a countdown to the next step, the "prize": college acceptance and high school graduation. Those four years of high school were probably an uphill climb, with each successive year getting more challenging academically as your workload increased and the course content in your classes broadened. Simultaneously, you were expected to juggle standardized testing, push yourself to enroll in advanced classes, pass your exams, visit colleges, and complete college applications. You needed to get through all these small milestones in order to reach the finish line of your secondary education: college acceptance. There is a reason you might be tired. And you have succeeded.

You'll be happy to know that college is *not* the same game. You're aiming to graduate in four years, but you are *not* gearing up for another high school–like race to the finish line. You're in your new college environment to live, learn, and grow.

INTRODUCING YOURSELF TO OTHERS

In chapter 2, you'll read our tips for connecting with your new roommate(s) before you meet and important things to discuss with them before you move in together. But what about the other students you will meet during pre-orientation, orientation, and when you arrive on campus? If meeting new peers does not come naturally to you, here are some great tips:

- **BOND OVER SHARED TRANSITION-TO-COLLEGE EXPERIENCES,** such as your travel to college, your residence hall, the food on campus, or a mandatory program you have attended together.

- **BE ON TIME AND DRESS APPROPRIATELY AT YOUR FIRST HALL MEETING.** Don't be *that* kid—the one who shows up late and interrupts the RA's orientation; you'll leave your peers with the impression that you haven't totally bought into community living.

- **DON'T DOUBT YOURSELF.** Don't forget that you belong at your school. You've earned your spot in the first-year class, just like everyone else.

- **THINK ABOUT HOW MUCH YOU ARE CONTRIBUTING TO A CONVERSATION.** When you're nervous, it's easy to speak more than is necessary. Remember to listen and respond to your new peers during conversation just as much as you speak.

- **GET INVOLVED AND ATTEND AS MUCH PROGRAMMING AS YOU CAN HANDLE.** The first week or two of college should be an overview of campus for new students, so push yourself to check out everything. Following that, you can narrow your focus to the people and activities that suit you.

- **DON'T BE A KNOW-IT-ALL.** Remember that everyone you meet had the intellect to be accepted by your school. Instead, work on being a good listener.

- **ASK FOR HELP WHEN YOU NEED IT.** There are faculty, professional staff, student staff, and upper-class students who will be happy to give you directions if you're lost on campus or answer your newbie questions. Remember that after a few months at school, you'll be a student on campus who is able to help others.

- **CHECK OUT ACADEMIC DEPARTMENTS AND EVENTS THAT INTEREST YOU *EVEN IF YOU ARE UNSURE WHAT YOUR MAJOR WILL BE*.** Professionals in specialty academic fields and students who are concentrating their studies in a particular department are the best resources around. Telling someone "I'm a first-year student and thinking about majoring in . . ." will take you far.

- **TRY NOT TO WORRY, EVEN IF YOU FEEL INSECURE.** Every transition takes time. Think of how big and strange your middle school or high school felt when you first arrived. Feeling free of undue stress is one of the most important elements of preparation for your first week of college. There are many resources to turn to on campus if your stress does feel overwhelming, including your RA (chapter 2), the counseling center (chapter 10), or a peer leader (chapter 13).

- **GIVE NEW PEERS THE BENEFIT OF THE DOUBT.** Chances are, they're nervous as well. If your first impression of someone you meet is less than favorable, commit to giving them a second chance, but don't waste a ton of time forging friendships with people who don't share your values.

- **ASSUME THAT THERE *WILL* BE CHALLENGES.** Try not to put too much pressure on yourself to succeed in everything new you try. College is hard and often overwhelming; stress and fatigue add to the challenges. If you assume that baseline stress and worry are normative, you won't be so hard on yourself when social or academic situations seem tough.

Here Are Some Differences:

	HIGH SCHOOL	COLLEGE
YOUR IDENTITY	Usually tied to the activities you have engaged in	More complex and nuanced; tied to your social connections, course of study, and career aspirations
CHOOSING ACTIVITIES	Might be a strategy for college acceptance	To find a peer group, learn new skills, and enhance your lived experience
DEMONSTRATION OF "SUCCESS"	Standardized: GPA, test scores, hours of community service, leadership roles	Variable: Individualized and based on academic interests and career aspirations
INSTRUCTORS JUDGE YOU BY . . .	What you know and what knowledge you retain	The questions you ask

LEARNING TO SPEND TIME BY YOURSELF

It's impossible and unhealthy to take on every new college experience with a friend by your side. As you grow and develop into an adult, it's crucial to allow yourself to think freely, form opinions, and embrace the freedom you have to its fullest. This is often challenging for a first-year student, especially if you were raised with siblings. For some, spending hours alone feels like a waste of time; for others, it might even be anxiety-provoking. Please trust that spending time alone is an important skill to have in college, and the summer before you transition to campus is a great time to appreciate how different a new experience can be if you take it on by yourself.

You hear a lot about how college is a time to develop close friendships, and that is absolutely true. But it's also an important time to appreciate being by yourself. In high school, that might have meant just staying in, watching Netflix, eating a sandwich, and waiting for your family to get home. We're not talking about that. We're talking about *really* having new experiences by yourself. This is a crucial skill, especially when you live in a residence hall, as there aren't many places to actually be alone, and the constant presence of other people where you sleep, eat, and even shower can get a bit overwhelming. If you're successful at this skill, you might even begin to welcome staying in on an occasional Friday night or heading out by yourself to have a new experience on a Saturday afternoon.

> In college, taking time each day to be alone, even thirty minutes to take a walk or just sit and think, is helpful. College is a lot more work than high school, and the stakes are higher, but remembering to stop, slow down, and spend some time focusing on yourself is a necessity for success.
>
> —COLLEGE STUDENT

SEEK INDEPENDENCE
(AND OWN THE RESPONSIBILITY THAT COMES WITH IT)

The summer before you head to campus is a great time to become independent in many areas of your life.

Some important things you should learn to do before leaving for college:

- Do your laundry (learn to separate colors from whites, and what needs to be air-dried)
- Change your sheets and make your bed
- Make your own medical appointments and renew your own prescriptions
- Iron your clothes
- Sew on a button
- Purchase tickets to events, for air travel, and for public transportation
- Read a bus schedule
- Pay an appropriate tip at a restaurant or coffee shop
- Set an alarm (or alarms) to get up and out of your room on time
- Manage your personal finances, including money transfers
- Mail a package and an envelope
- Register to vote and/or request and submit an absentee ballot
- Read nutrition labels on food
- Locate and use local businesses (dry cleaner, hair salon/barber shop)
- Purchase used textbooks
- Read unit prices to find cost-effective food
- Write a professional email
- Leave a professional voice mail
- Clean shared spaces (sinks, floors, minifridge, microwave, and other surfaces)

DO BEFORE YOU GO

Practice relying on yourself. Find two free hours before you leave for college to spend completely alone trying something new. Suggestions include a trip to a new neighborhood, museum, zoo, park, movie theater, or college campus.

Avoid your phone. Don't talk, text, or use social media during these hours, unless there is an emergency. Just be alone and spend time with the person you'll need to rely upon most in college: you.

Remember to keep your expectations (and the expectations that others have of you) reasonable. No one goes from dependent to independent overnight, and there is no doubt that you will make some mistakes along the way. If you lose your student ID, accidentally bleach a load of colored laundry, oversleep and miss a class, or have to call home for support more than you would like, remember that you are still learning how to college and how to be an adult. We promise your college professors all made similar mistakes when they were first-year students.

Being independent does *not* mean never seeking help. As a matter of fact, truly being an adult means being willing to find and use resources (either on campus or from your support system at home) when you need them. It also means making healthy choices (this is discussed in depth in chapter 9). With your new independence comes new responsibility as well. Sure, you *can* stay up all night with friends, but if you have class or work the next day, is that a smart decision?

Can you count how many times in the past someone at home reminded you to do your homework, clean your room, or take out the trash? At college, that someone is you—or no one (but if you wait long enough to change your sheets or do your laundry, it might remind you in its own scary way).

Foundations of Self

Although your experience in college will change your perspective about a whole host of things (and you should open yourself to new opinions—that's what college is all about), it's important not to lose track of your core values. They will ground the decisions you will have to make and prepare you to thrive in your college environment. As cliché as it sounds, don't be someone who is swayed by the masses or by popular opinion. You be you.

College is most likely the first time that you will live without your immediate family over an extended period of time, and lots of people think *that* is the toughest transition. We would argue that what is the most challenging for first-year students is realizing that you are at a point in your life where you have to stop doing things just to please your family, and instead start doing what is best for you and your future. That is a step toward being an adult. Establishing your independence really means learning to take care of yourself, and this is an ongoing process.

COMMUNICATING WITH YOUR FAMILY:
EACH SITUATION IS UNIQUE

Your daily interaction with your family will (and should) be altered when you leave for college. With preparation, you can avoid what often turns out to be a significant source of conflict between new college students and the people they've left at home. While there really isn't a "normal" college student–to–home communication formula, it's important to discuss both sets of expectations—yours and your family's—and it's crucial to find a plan that works for everyone's needs.

The communication arrangement you make will be unique to you and your family. Some first-year college students and their parents talk or text multiple times a day, and others talk or text weekly. Others report that they talk on the phone infrequently, but text often. Some video chat with their families each week, and others don't at all. The communication varies by schedule (and sometimes time difference), limited privacy, and family members' comfort in exploring options beyond the traditional phone call.

Social media can make it easier to let your family know what you've been up to, but it comes with its own challenges of appropriateness and privacy. It's important to note that there are also special circumstances: not everyone has an open and communicative relationship with their family. Some first-year students come from divorced, multigenerational, or multilingual families, which may complicate communication or the time it takes to check in with all parties.

Concerns from the Home Front

Remember that it isn't all about your needs. Your family has dedicated years to raising you, and they aren't going to turn off their concern about you when you move out. You won't be around for them to see you regularly, so they will want to know how you are doing while you're away from home. It will be crucial to take on a more conscious role as a conduit for that information.

This doesn't mean you need to share every detail of your life, but your family will expect and appreciate some type of regular update in whatever format you decide upon together. They will want to hear some stories about your new routine, and it's your responsibility to share some. Be prepared for them to ask you *a lot* of questions in the beginning (and these might seem annoying). When they do reach out, it probably isn't because they want to interfere, but because you haven't been communicative enough for their needs. And if you call your family when you are homesick, upset, or in need, don't forget to contact them again when you're feeling better or more in control so they'll feel better, too.

Balancing Independence and Communication with Your Family

First-year students need and require independence to successfully transition from home to college. "Adulting" involves taking responsibility for your own life as you figure out your goals, make mistakes, revel in your new accomplishments, and compromise on a communication strategy with your family. If it would make your mom feel good to receive a smiling photo of you and your roommate, send one. If you know your grandfather would "know" that you were safe if he just heard your voice, make the effort to call him. If your younger sibling needs good-night texts to adjust after you've left home, it's pretty easy to send them.

> As much as you like to think that you have finally found your freedom and you're away from your family, you will still need them. Tell them a few details about your week and ask them how life is back home. Even if you do not feel homesick, you should make the effort to call.
> —COLLEGE STUDENT

Flexible Communication Relationships

You'll probably have to adjust your phone or video chat schedule once you get a better idea of what your college life looks like. For example, you might have agreed to video chat with your family every Sunday evening, but then you join an organization that meets at that time. Maybe you miss your siblings more than you expected to (hey, stop laughing!), or they have a harder time with you being away than they thought (now tell *them* to stop laughing). As long as you respect each other's needs and time, you'll be able to build a communication plan that works for everyone.

YOU'RE NOT AN IMPOSTER OR AN EXPERT—BE AN EXPLORER

I had all sorts of preconceived notions about sounding like that annoying first-year student with stupid questions and that my professors would be frustrated with me taking up their time. In reality, my ideas could not have been more wrong.

—COLLEGE STUDENT

As professors, we often hear that our students feel like *imposters*. They're intimidated by their peers. They tell us that their classmates seem to know everything and that they're embarrassed to ask a question in class. When we ask where they got this idea, students tell us that their classmates are more confident and certain, argue passionately in residence hall lounges and at meals, or learned all about the material in their internships. In college, we call this "imposter syndrome." It can discourage students from speaking up, seeking help, or sharing what they know.

On the other hand, some students say they are *experts*. When we ask why, they tell us they volunteered on a political campaign, interned in a law office, or did a service trip abroad. They express confidence that they know a lot more than their peers. The "expert trap" comes with its own dangers. Our "expert" students are often surprised at their first paper grades, when they learn that college writing isn't about confidently asserting a preexisting opinion. Neither of these mind-sets—imposter or expert—is a healthy approach to college work.

In reality, although some students come to college more prepared than others, a first-year student "expert" is quite rare. (An exception, in our experience, is our military veteran students who are beginning their education after years of specialized military service. However, we find that their work prepares them to accept expert advice when approaching a new discipline—a mind-set worth emulating.) It's important to go into college with more questions than answers; push yourself to ask questions and be excited about finding the answers. As a college student, you're not an imposter or an expert; you should be an explorer.

DO BEFORE YOU GO

Practice saying, "I don't know." It is the most accurate answer in the world, but people go to great lengths to avoid saying it. Take note of the times when you really *don't* know but say something like, "I'm not really sure, maybe it's . . . ," and instead make an effort to just say, "I don't know." You can start with people who you trust on topics that you're not embarrassed to say you don't know. For example, say it when a sibling asks you a question about a sport they follow that you don't, or your parent mentions something particular to their job that you don't understand.

Self-Assessment

To get ready to enter college with an explorer's mind-set, take some time to consider whether the following statements apply to you. You might want to free-write about them or discuss them with a parent.

- I worry that my classmates will know more than I do. (imposter)

- I think my new classmates are going to look to me as one of the most knowledgeable people. (expert)

- I'm not comfortable raising my hand to ask a question. (imposter, worried about seeming inferior; or expert, worried image among peers will be destroyed)

- When someone else asks a question, they seem unprepared. (expert)

- I am comfortable not knowing everything about a subject. (explorer)

- I find difficult questions exciting. (explorer)

- I'm uncomfortable when I feel like other people know more than I do. (imposter)

Are you starting with an expert's mind-set, an imposter's mind-set, or an explorer's mind-set?

How to Avoid Imposter Syndrome:

1. Remember your professor isn't grading you on your high school work or internships; she's looking at your performance in her class.

2. Look at course prerequisites in the course catalog. If the class has no prerequisites, that means any student is considered prepared to take it.

3. Remember that your college admissions office determined you were ready to be a first-year student there.

4. Think about your high school experience. Remember that there were some quiet people who had a lot to teach you and some know-it-alls who didn't.

How to Avoid the Expert Trap:

1. Your course syllabus or the course catalog will often include "learning objectives." These are the goals for the course. They can include skills such as arguing both sides of an issue or subject matter such as differential equations or the federal system of government. Review those learning outcomes. If you think you are already fairly accomplished, ask yourself how you could get to the next level.

2. Consider the course subject matter and identify things you *don't* know. You might have studied the US Congress as a member of your high school's debate team, but what do you still have to learn about Congress? Write down a list of questions you will challenge yourself to answer.

3. Think about how proud you felt the day you learned you were accepted to college. Now remember that everyone else in your class was accepted, too.

4. Read your professor's bio on the school website and consider their publications, research, and education. Identify some subjects about which you'd like to know more, and plan to ask your professor about those subjects during office hours.

How to Approach Your Classes as an Explorer:

1. Consider the reasons you are going to college, including your future career goals. You might be a very prepared first-year student, but that is only the beginning. Imagine what it will take to get from where you are to where you want to be after college. Look at every class as an opportunity to fill in the gaps between where you are and where you need to go.

2. Listen to your classmates and challenge yourself to consider their ideas.

Myth vs. Fact	
MYTH	**FACT**
Saying "I don't know" makes you look like a bad student.	Understanding what you don't know—and being excited to find out—makes you a great student.
Some of your classmates are experts—and you're already way behind.	You are all at the beginning of your higher-education career. Some people might have an AP course or internship under their belt, but you're all first-year students.

The most confident and opinionated students are the most accomplished.	An opinion is not an accomplishment, and loud does not equal right. Reading, listening, challenging yourself, and responding to challenges are accomplishments.
Being a great student is about finding arguments to support your opinions.	Great students explore difficult texts, ideas, and arguments in order to form educated opinions.

YOUR VOICE: CIVIL DISCOURSE

Your voice is like your laundry and your budget—it's *your* responsibility. In college, you have more freedom to speak your mind than ever before (and possibly ever after—your employer might not let you have political arguments with clients or wear a "F—the Patriarchy" T-shirt in the office). How you use this freedom is your decision, and it's an important one. The new college you will be known by your voice. So how will you use it?

FAST FACT

Private universities have more power to restrict free speech than public ones. However, most universities have strong policies protecting freedom of speech.

When we talk about speech, we spend more time talking about rights than responsibilities. In the United States, freedom of speech is protected by the First Amendment to our Constitution. Universities have a special concern about freedom of speech: in particular, if professors couldn't share unpopular ideas without fear of punishment, innovation wouldn't be possible. Student activists have also fought for the freedom to express unpopular ideas.

The question of what you *can* say on campus is a pretty easy one. There are some common rules that colleges apply that probably won't surprise you:

1. **LIMITATIONS ON THE TIME, PLACE, AND MANNER.** Quiet hours in residence hells; quiet study areas (such as the library); and rules about where you can post leaflets and whether you can chalk university property.

2. **DISRUPTIONS OF EDUCATIONAL PROCESS.** Your school will ensure that your speech doesn't interfere with other people's educational opportunities. For example, you might not be able to use a megaphone for your political protest near a classroom building when classes are in session.

3. **THREATS.** Threats are not protected speech under the First Amendment. In fact, it can be a crime to threaten others.

4. **HARASSMENT.** Harassment is behavior (including speech) that demeans or harms others, creating a hostile environment. People often disagree about what constitutes harassment, but here's one rule to live by: if a person tells you that your conduct is unwanted or unwelcome, stop immediately.

Unless you are going to college to use a megaphone during classes or deface property, these rules shouldn't affect your life too much. But how will you use your freedom? In using a voice that will serve your goals, it's helpful to strive for speech that is:

- **TRUTHFUL.** Injecting falsehood into a public dialogue or sharing a falsehood with one listener does not serve the listener.

- **PRODUCTIVE.** It achieves a goal that we set for ourselves or a service we would like to offer our communities. This includes things like:
  - Informing our listeners of a fact that is relevant to the conversation.
  - Introducing nuance about a topic where the listener feels certainty.
  - Critiquing an existing idea or claim (but not the person who made it).

- Introducing a question for which we genuinely want or need an answer (this is not the same as generating a controversy based on falsehoods—e.g., if climate change is real).
- Sharing a personal perspective that could help your listener(s) communicate with you more effectively or better understand your concerns.
- Bringing joy and connection through humor.

- **AUDIENCE-CENTERED.** Speech and expression are communication. Effective and productive communicators attempt to connect with the listener. An audience-centered speaker:

  - Learns their audience's level of familiarity with the topic and communicates accordingly.
  - Offers facts and perspectives that the speaker can verify, but does not try to "educate" the audience about who *they* are.
  - Is respectful of the audience's time and goals. For example, in a classroom, an audience-centered speaker would respond directly to the professor's question rather than introducing an unrelated topic that does not serve the course's learning objectives.
  - Considers the listeners' perspectives, including whether certain topics or language are painful or offensive.
  - Verifies that the conversation partner is open to hearing something. For example, in the residence hall, an audience-centered speaker might not approach a fellow student who is studying and start asking them questions about their identity or politics.

- **FOCUSED ON LISTENING CIVILLY AND PRODUCTIVELY.** Civil and productive listening:

  - Means we listen to understand, not only to respond. For example, if we raise our hand before a classmate has finished speaking, we are not listening to understand her whole point but rather to rebut that point.
  - Leads us to ask questions before offering rebuttals.
  - Aligns with our goals for education: to become more knowledgeable, understand others' perspectives, appreciate

nuance, and develop our critical thinking by acknowledging and engaging with the gaps in our claims.

- Mirrors our expectations of our own listeners.
- Reflects our values, including decisions about when *not* to listen (when told that three is larger than five or that we are inferior to others).

■ **OUR OWN RESPONSIBILITY:**

- Only we can decide whether our speech will reflect our values, serve our goals, or benefit our communities.
- Our choice of what to say can have consequences, including that others might not be persuaded, members of our community might disagree with us, or we might not meet academic standards. For example, if you invite a speaker to campus who has a record of disparaging Jews, you must be prepared to hear Jewish students say that you have given anti-Semitism a platform.

DO BEFORE YOU GO

Examine your habits as a speaker and listener and your goals for your education. Set some goals for how you will communicate and listen. Consider these questions and write or type your responses:

1. **What do you hope to achieve in college**
   - In the classroom?
   - In your campus community?
   - In the community beyond campus?
   - In preparing for your career (and the jobs and internships you hold while in college)?

2. **How can you use your voice to serve those goals?**
   - I can advance my career goals by doing / avoiding _____
   - To show my peers who I am, I want to _____
   - I will learn more in my classes by _____

3. **What kinds of communication do you consider productive? How about unproductive? Try filling in the blanks:**

   - I'm more likely to hear someone out if they _____ [examples: treat me with respect, use terms I understand, listen to me]
   - I'd probably choose not to engage with someone again if they _____ [examples: attacked me personally, insulted my identity, shouted, interrupted me repeatedly]

4. **As of now, what kind of speaker are you?**

   - Do you challenge *ideas* or attack *people?*
   - Do you pay attention to your audience in deciding how to communicate?
   - How careful are you to share only what you know to be true? Do you quote from news articles that turn out to be fake?
   - If you share something that turns out to be false or offensive, do you correct the record or apologize?

5. **As of now, what kind of listener are you?**

   - Do you listen to understand or only to rebut?
   - Do you ever changed your mind once you've heard another perspective?
   - Do you seek out different perspectives and opinions, whether in conversation or in your reading choices?

   Now pick some goals for your speaking and listening.

   - I want to become a better listener. To do that, I plan to [examples: decide not to raise my hand in class one day and to take notes on what my peers say]
   - I plan to interrupt less. To help achieve that goal I will _____.
   - I need to get more comfortable with different perspectives. I will _____ [examples: attend an event hosted by a political group with which I disagree; have a respectful conversation with someone of a different religion; read an article by a columnist with whom I often disagree; research opposing arguments about a political idea that's important to me]

An important part of transitioning to college is learning about yourself as you take on more responsibility away from home. That means navigating your relationship with your family as you seek independence in your new surroundings. In the next chapter, you'll incorporate what we've introduced here—defining your identity and finding your voice—into discussions about getting to know your new roommate(s), learning from differences, and navigating potential conflict in this new and important relationship.

2

DOUBLING (OR TRIPLING) DOWN: SHARING YOUR LIVING SPACE

The whole idea of sharing a pretty small living space with someone else is probably at least a little bit unsettling. However, living with a roommate can also be one of the most important college experiences you will have, and you'll learn a lot about yourself and others in the process.

—COLLEGE STUDENT

LIVING WITH A ROOMMATE

Living with a roommate (or roommates) is an exciting and sometimes simultaneously challenging experience. Many first-year college students assume they'll instantly connect with their roommate(s), and in many situations, this does happen. However, *expecting* your first college roommate to be a lifelong best friend might set you up for disappointment.

That said, it's important to put work into this relationship because your roommate can be the key to a positive residential experience for your first semester. Instead of trying to be best friends, we suggest that you work toward being best roommates. Try to focus on creating a friendly relationship built on trust, appreciation for your similarities and differences, and acceptance of everyone's approaches to living. There are many ways to be "best roommates." Finding the one that works for you will take time, but it's worth it.

Questions many incoming college students have that are expected and normal:

- Will this person like me? Will I like them?

- How will we communicate if we have issues?

- What if we don't have much in common?

- What will it be like to live in close proximity to a stranger?

- How will it feel if my roommate connects to friends/classes/activities more quickly than I do?

- Should I disclose personal information about myself (and if so, when)?

- What is appropriate to ask my new roommate about their life and experiences?

Reach Out in Advance, but Think About Your First Conversation Carefully

Most US colleges and universities provide housing information and inform you of your roommate(s) match four to six weeks in advance of move-in day. Whether you chose your roommate or your school chose them for you, it's a good idea to reach out in advance.

Although you should provide an accurate description of your habits and passions, don't share too much too soon. You have time; you'll be living with your roommate for the next nine months. If you can arrange an in-person meeting or one by video chat or phone, this is ideal. Do your best to relax and share information that you feel is important and relevant to a living situation and save the deeper life discussions for later. Even if you're nervous, try to be yourself. Facades aren't helpful (and your roommate will figure out the real you in the near future). Most important, remember that your new roommate is probably nervous as well.

Tips for the Incoming College Student About Your School's Roommate Questionnaire

You Shouldn't:

- Answer the questions about your cleanliness, bedtime, and study habits based on your aspirational self.

- Expect to be paired with a roommate who shares the same demographic background and life experiences as yours.

- Allow a parent to fill out the questionnaire for you, even if they say they know you best or it saves you time.

You Should:

- Tell the truth about your daily routines, both good and not so good, at this point in time.

- Expect to be paired with someone quite different from yourself, but who has similar living habits.

- Fill out the questionnaire yourself, then ask someone who has lived with you for confirmation about the way(s) you have assessed yourself.

KNOW BEFORE YOU GO

If the information has not been provided, ask the residence life/housing office at your school for a suggested packing list, the layout and square footage of your room, and a list of the items (such as a vacuum) that your residence hall provides for students.

You might consider discussing the expectations for your shared space and the items you are bringing to college that you might share, such as:

- TV
- Microwave

- Rug
- Couch or chair
- Popcorn popper
- Electric kettle
- Minifridge
- Fan
- Dust pan and broom
- Cleaning supplies

Ask your roommate questions related to sharing a living space. For example:

- "Do you think you'll have overnight guests?"
- "How would you describe your neatness?"
- "What are your study habits?"
- "What type of music do you listen to?"
- "What time do you usually go to bed?"
- "What is your morning routine?"

Be honest with your answers as well. You can't cover everything in one conversation, but even this first meeting is an opportunity for you to begin to voice concerns, share your opinions, and ultimately compromise if there is a disagreement. Most important, try not to judge this first dialogue if it doesn't go the way you would have liked; all relationships take time to grow and strengthen.

The discussion topics that follow will most likely be addressed after you and your roommate(s) have become comfortable with each other. The way someone identifies (for example, as male, biracial, atheist, dyslexic) is personal, and will often be disclosed if and when individuals deem the relationship to be safe.

The first time you connect with your roommate(s), consider discussing:

- Hometowns and high school experiences
- Hobbies/interests
- Summer job/plans
- Intended major
- Co-curricular activities in which you hope to participate
- Knowledge of your new college town and campus
- Expectations of your living arrangement
- What each of you is bringing to the room
- Family, siblings, pets
- Excitement and fears about moving to school
- Significant others/relationships

The first time you connect with your roommate(s), don't ask them to discuss:

- Political affiliation
- Family jobs/income/social class
- Religion/faith/spirituality
- Mental/physical health
- Sexual orientation
- Gender identity
- Disabilities
- Race/ethnic identity
- Documented status of family

Social Media

You probably know how easy it is to be misrepresented online. Following, friending, or adding your new roommate(s) on social media is totally appropriate and often expected. Remember that people carefully select the photos they post on social media, so these will be filtered and edited images, just like yours might be. Try hard not to judge your new roommate(s) based on what they share on social media; do your best not to formulate opinions about them before you meet in person. Your new roommate and others who find you through your incoming class correspondence will be looking at your social media as well.

If you have met in person or by video chat before arriving on campus, seeing your roommate(s) for the first time should be less awkward. There are a few other things to discuss before move-in day to create a calmer experience for everyone who sets foot in your new (and probably quite small) room. You can't always control the situation, but knowing what to expect on move-in day will ease the stress.

AVOIDING MOVE-IN DAY DRAMA

Moving in can be a stressful time for everyone involved. Communicating clearly with family, new roommate(s), and campus staff is important and can help the move-in process go a bit more smoothly. Keeping an open mind is also essential, as first impressions aren't always accurate. Finally, maintaining a sense of humor and having some fun during move-in makes the experience more positive for everyone.

—RESIDENCE LIFE DIRECTOR

Roommates don't always arrive on campus at the same time. Ask your roommate what their schedule will be so that you'll know what to expect. Sometimes one student gets to campus earlier, perhaps because they are an international student, a student athlete, or arriving for a specialized program. Showing up to an empty room feels different from showing up to one in which someone has already been living for days or even weeks. Tell each other who (if anyone) will accompany you, what the expectations of your respective families will be for move-in, and what your plans are for their departure.

CARING FOR YOUR SHARED SPACE

Your room will never again look so organized, neat, and clean as it does on move-in day. But what about a week later? Defining "clean" is something you and your roommate(s) will need to do together. Think about whether you will split cleaning tasks or pick a day of the week (such as Sunday evening) for a regular cleanup and trash removal. Many residence life offices suggest or require a roommate contract or agreement to hold all parties responsible for their own conduct. There will be other items that you'll need to discuss once you have found your roommate groove together, such as:

- Which personal items are off-limits and which possessions can be shared?

- What rules for locking your door make both of you feel secure (see chapter 11)

- How hosting visitors and overnight guests will work in your shared space (including handling hook-ups and being "sexiled")

- If you will establish rules for noise (music, alarms, and talking on the phone)
- How you will accommodate your differing schedules (wake-up time, classes, studying, social time, and sleep time/length)

DO BEFORE YOU GO

Talk to your roommate about the following related to move-in day:

- What time will each of you arrive on campus for move-in?
- How will you pick beds/sides of the room and decide to set up the space?
- If you're moving in on the same date/time of day, would your families (or one family and the roommate(s)) consider spending some time together to talk or share a meal?

CARING FOR YOURSELF, YOUR ROOMMATE, AND OTHERS IN YOUR RESIDENCE HALL

It's one thing to set up a list of ground rules about your shared space, but there are more complex parts of living in such close proximity to other human beings and sharing common spaces with them. Here are some really important things to think about before heading off to campus:

- **DAILY COMMUNICATION** is of utmost importance. A thoughtful gesture, a smile, or a word of encouragement on a rough day goes a long way. Remember to follow up with the other person to ask how an exam or challenging situation went.

- **COMMON COURTESY** is a requirement of a successful roommate relationship. This includes cleaning up after yourself, making the effort to engage frequently with others, and being inclusive and welcoming in open spaces.

- **ACKNOWLEDGING INDIVIDUAL NEEDS** can help ease worry. Whether your roommates or hall mates need help with something disability-related they have disclosed, have a condition that needs medication or daily management, or are just temporarily ill, try to be supportive in a manner they welcome.

- **BE THOUGHTFUL ABOUT SOCIOECONOMIC DIFFERENCES AND ACCESS TO MONEY.** Chances are, students in your residence hall have come from varied backgrounds. Don't make assumptions about what they can/cannot afford, whether it is ordering take-out food, going to a movie, or purchasing something for your shared space.

- **CONFLICT RESOLUTION** is an important skill you'll need in the workforce, and living in a residence hall is a great place to develop it. Listen more than you speak, be thoughtful and open-minded in expressing your opinions, and work on compromising as much as possible. Remember that different people have different experiences with communication about conflict. Don't forget that your residence life staff is trained to help out if needed.

Differentiating Between Normative and Potentially Dangerous Behaviors and Feelings

Now for some serious talk. When you are living in close proximity to your college peers, you will become up-close observers of others. It's important to note that college experiences and the feelings related to them might play out quite differently for each college student. Learn about these distinctions and what to watch for before you arrive on campus.

Most behaviors you observe in other students and the thoughts and feelings that they express are considered **normative**. They are a regular part of the exploration, development, and stress experienced in college. You can help a friend by voicing your concerns about their behavior or offering support, advice, or simply listening to their worries if you feel comfortable doing so.

However, if you observe **potentially dangerous** behaviors or hear about thoughts and feelings that sound like a person is at risk, you should refer them to a professional as soon as possible. Remember that while you are neither your friend's caretaker nor a trained mental health professional, you can play a *very* important role in identifying a student in distress. Without question, you should refer the person of concern to a staff member who is trained to guide students to the appropriate college resource where they can receive the assistance they need.

NORMATIVE BEHAVIORS/ FEELINGS	POTENTIALLY DANGEROUS BEHAVIORS/FEELINGS
Stress: Normal emotional anxiety, pressure, tension, or worry; part of a typical college student's life	**Distress: A state of trouble, risk, or peril; an extreme emotional feeling of suffering, pain, sorrow, or panic**
Feeling uncomfortable: Normal fear of moving outside one's comfort zone; productive feeling for learning and growth	**Feeling unsafe: Physical or emotional danger or threat of impending physical or emotional danger**

GETTING TO KNOW YOUR RESIDENCE HALL STAFF

Every campus has a team hired to work with your residence experience. No matter what their titles may be at your school, know that there will be professional and student staff to help with your transition and needs. You will most likely have a resident adviser (RA—also called a senior resident, resident assistant, house fellow, resident mentor, peer adviser, etc.), who is a trained peer leader and mentors a group of students in a residence hall. This is usually an upper-class student who can serve as a resource, answer institutional questions, plan programs, build community, help students make connections to groups on campus, and enforce policies.

Your RA will most likely report to a graduate student or other live-in professional staff member of the residence life/housing office. This person, your resident director (RD—also called a community director, residence hall director, or residence life coordinator), is most likely enrolled in a master's program or has a master's degree in college student personnel or student development. They are responsible for managing a larger residential area—perhaps an entire residence hall or series of them. This person usually provides on-call emergency support after hours; oversees front-desk staff; and has been extensively trained to work with undergraduate students.

Be mindful that the unsung heroes of the residence halls are the team who make sure that your common spaces, such as lounges, kitchens, and bathrooms, are kept clean. As an adult, you should do your best to clean up after yourself every day. It's also important as a member of a community to make every effort to say hello and routinely thank these individuals for taking care of your new living space.

PRO-TIP

Both your RA and RD will be a great resource if you are struggling with feeling overwhelmed, homesick, nervous, frustrated, or insecure academically or socially, which many first-year college students experience.

***

The next chapter moves the discussion from relationships with roommates, hall mates, and staff inside your residence hall to your communication with the larger population of students on your campus. We will talk about common misconceptions of first-year college students, including FOMO (fear of missing out) and making assumptions about others. We will also offer tips for juggling high school and college friendships, and the benefits of thinking and learning outside your comfort zone.

3

BEYOND ICEBREAKERS: GETTING TO KNOW YOUR COLLEGE PEERS

Being uprooted from the life you know and having to make a whole new group of friends can be stressful, and it's very easy to just cling to the first person you get along with. Friendships are meant to be systems of mutual respect and support.

—COLLEGE STUDENT

MORE THAN A STATISTIC: A SNAPSHOT OF YOUR COLLEGE CLASSMATES

You've likely been looking at numbers and statistics about colleges throughout the application process. Maybe you can even recite the acceptance rates and SAT/ACT score ranges of several schools at this point. Chances are, you spent hours studying how your high school GPA compared to that of others applying to the same colleges. The good news is, that is all behind you.

Now that you are about to become a college student, there are other numbers and statistics that matter much more. If you are like most college students, you have come from a fairly (if not very) homogeneous hometown and have interacted with others who look alike, come from a similar economic class, and maybe even share a race, ethnicity, or religion. You might have been a part of that homogeneous group, and you might not have been.

KNOW BEFORE YOU GO

The first step to interacting with others unlike yourself is knowing how your new classmates identify. The following are questions for you to look up on your school website so that you are more knowledgeable about the student population of your college before you arrive:

Demographic diversity at your school:

- What percentage of students identify as persons of color?
- With which religions do the students identify?
- What percentage of undergraduates receive financial aid?
- What is the male-to-female ratio?
- What percent of students identify as transgender or gender nonbinary (and is this number easily accessible)?
- What is the age range of undergraduate students?
- How many students come from out of state? What are the largest feeder states?
- How many countries are represented by the international students?
- How many of your classmates are the first in their families to attend college?

MAKING NEW COLLEGE FRIENDS

It's important to understand that making friends in college is challenging for many first-year students. Just forget all those TV shows and movies where people meet their best friends on move-in day. Although we hope that you relate well to your roommate, your hall mates, or those in an orientation group in your first few days on campus, don't expect those folks to be your closest companions all semester long. You (or they) might find better friendship connections with other people. Although you should try hard not to judge people the first time you meet them, even if they say something that irritates you, trust your gut instincts. Don't be afraid to branch out if the people you are hanging out with engage in behaviors or conversations that aren't for you.

Most important, keep your expectations reasonable: your first year is for truly learning about yourself and others. Making real, close friendships takes *time*. Don't forget that many of your friends from home are people you have known for years. You'll have more free time in college than you did in high school because of the reduced number of classes, so use it well. The wait for a close-knit friend group will be worth it. Don't forget that the majority of your incoming first-year peers share similar concerns about finding their "people." Most will be thrilled if you reach out and connect with them.

Four easy ways to meet friends during your first semester

- **IN YOUR RESIDENCE HALL:** Keep your room door open (if it's okay with your roommate) and hang out in your floor lounge or kitchen to begin meeting others.

- **IN CLASSES:** Introduce yourself to the people sitting next to you. It feels dorky at first, but chances are, people in some of your classes will share a major or similar academic interest.

- **IN CLUBS, ORGANIZATIONS, AND AFFINITY GROUPS:** These are groups that draw people with similar interests or identities (more on this in chapter 18). Attend meetings and events early in your first semester and be as outgoing as you are comfortable.

- **OVER FOOD:** Everyone has to eat, and food is a great way to break down barriers. Ask someone from your residence hall or a class to a meal, a coffee, or a late-night pizza. Also, try to make an effort to chat with other students in food lines rather than looking at your phone.

FOMO

FOMO, or "fear of missing out," is a very real fear for many first-year students. FOMO is also the reason you see first-year college students traveling in packs of five to ten people, especially to meals. First-year students often express anxiety about being seen by themselves on campus. They are afraid that it will look like they don't have friends. There is even a recognition among first-year students that they would rather be with a group of people they don't particularly like than to be seen alone.

There is also another type of FOMO that includes fear of missing out on the excitement back home or at another school where several of your high school friends are enrolled and seem to be enjoying a great time together. This fear can be exacerbated by active social media usage. A study highlighted by *Time* magazine in 2016 found that those with strong FOMO consistently used social media upon waking up, during meals, and right before going to sleep at night.[i] An active social media presence is usually a positive experience for first-year college students, especially if it helps you connect with new groups of people on your campus. However, if you find yourself observing these harmful patterns where you are looking at others' social media accounts and feeling *left out*, make sure to set some boundaries for yourself.

College is about building new in-person relationships. Make a plan to limit your time on social media so it doesn't interfere with doing so. In preparation for your transition to campus, consider removing your social media apps from your phone or limiting notifications.

But What About Your High School Friends?

First-year students report that their efforts to keep up with friends from home by text, phone, or through social media have mixed results. While you might be excited to share stories of your new college relationships and hear your friends' stories, too, it is important to realize that everyone is going through their own transition, and some of those transitions are more challenging than others. Try not to judge high school friends who aren't as good at staying in touch as others. It is important to recognize that some students need to completely immerse themselves in their college experiences, while others are better juggling both home and college friends.

Remember as well that you're evolving in college, and so are your high school friends. You might stay close to your good friends and be excited to reconnect. It's hard for some first-year students to imagine that many of their high school friendships might even have changed by Thanksgiving or by winter break. Keep in touch with those important folks from home—perhaps video chat with them sometimes so they don't seem so far away—but don't live in the past. Make sure to invest fully in your new college relationships.

THINKING AND LEARNING OUTSIDE YOUR COMFORT ZONE

In chapter 18, we will encourage you to join clubs and organizations during your first semester to find your niche on campus. We have all been socialized to search out what is safe and familiar, and the majority of these groups will bring you that comfort and introduce you to the type of people you have encountered before. That early involvement is crucial to your college transition and will set you up to become an engaged member of your new campus community.

But college is also a time for you to push yourself outside what is easy and familiar. It's an opportunity to learn about differences of thought and experience and grow from that knowledge. Many first-year experience courses and seminars require students to seek new experiences outside their comfort zones, acknowledging the importance of the activity for personal and intellectual growth.

Going into college my freshman year, I thought I knew exactly who I was—a Jewish Studies major. However, I could not have imagined the results that came from stepping out of my comfort zone. Operating a light board was something I decided to do last minute in a pinch when a Shakespearean theater troupe on campus needed someone, and I needed something I'd never done before for a First Year Experience class assignment. I had stage managed productions in high school, but never dared to touch the light board. I dove right in and formed a connection with a senior who taught me everything I needed to know. After days of fader moving, level changing, gel peeling, and cord plugging, I had rigged and programmed lights for an entire show. I gained a lot of knowledge about colors, backgrounds, and programming, but most important, I found a space full of people who were able to support me in doing something I had never done before. Afterward, I went on to codesign another show with an older student. I ended up designing four shows total that year.

—COLLEGE STUDENT

Think for a minute about how much you would learn at a college lecture given by a professor whose field is completely unfamiliar to you. How about a discussion led by students who have a different political identification than yourself? What about cheering on your school at a sport you've never seen played, or listening to a student jazz quartet when you usually listen to country?

These are excellent ways to experience and learn about the differing lives and academic interests of the students on your campus. Trying things outside your zone of familiarity is another avenue of adulting. It will help you to expand your intellectual knowledge and better understand some of the diverse interests of your college peers.

DO BEFORE YOU GO

Before you leave for campus, find a free or cheap event in your hometown that is completely unfamiliar to you, such as:

- A lecture at a community college, local museum, or public library
- A religious service at a house of worship you have never entered
- An athletic competition of a sport you don't know how to play

Challenge yourself to attend the event, pushing outside what is comfortable and familiar, and see what the experience is like for you.

HOW TO AVOID MAKING ASSUMPTIONS
ABOUT OTHERS

Do you remember the saying, "Assuming makes an ASS out of U and ME"? This is also a great lesson for first-year college students, as well as a larger life lesson. Think about the demographic diversity of the students on your campus that you researched at the beginning of this chapter. It's one thing to know *about* people different from you with whom you share a campus, and another thing to meet (and hopefully form meaningful relationships) with them.

Interacting with a diverse group of peers with different life experiences is one of the most enriching parts of college. But the fact is, this part of your college experience might not always be easy or comfortable. What if you offend someone without meaning to? What if someone offends you? Most of us have been in new situations where our words, facial expressions, or actions had an impact on others that we didn't intend them to. And we've been on the other side, too, feeling hurt by someone whose intentions were good but whose words, actions, or facial expressions meant something different to us.

This most often occurs when we don't know the other person very well and we have made assumptions about their motives—or they have made assumptions about ours. This is a prejudgment . . . and prejudgment is the root of the word *prejudice*. We often make assumptions that other people think, feel, and experience life the same way we do. But social interactions are complicated, and a choice of words, tone of voice, look, or a gesture could be interpreted differently from how it was meant. Perhaps following an assumption about someone's motives, you begin to question the other person, analyze what you assume they are thinking, and criticize their next moves more harshly.

Prejudice can be based on a number of factors, including race, sex, age, gender, disability, sexual orientation, gender identity, nationality, socioeconomic status, or religion. It can have a strong influence on how people interact with others, particularly with those who are different from themselves. When people hold prejudicial attitudes, they often paint others of a particular identity (or those they *assume* hold that identity) with a broad brush without looking at the person as an individual. This can lead to stereotyping, bullying, and discrimination.

DO BEFORE YOU GO

Think back on a time when you believed that someone was mocking you or thought you were inferior in some way. Perhaps you made the assumption that someone's comment was condescending. What happened next?

- Think about your first thought or reaction at the time.
- Remember how you responded (or perhaps you were so hurt by those words or gesture that you didn't respond).
- Was your reaction driven by an assumption (or prejudgment) that they made about you? Was your reaction driven by an assumption (or prejudgment) that you made about them?

Wouldn't It Be Simpler Just to Ask?

During a negative interaction, we tend to jump to conclusions without asking the other person to explain their words or gestures. When you feel hurt or angry about a comment or facial expression sent your way, ask for clarification. You have the right to be direct, tell the person that you were hurt or annoyed by what they said or did, and ask them to explain. Asking questions about the other person's intent reduces the chance of misunderstandings in the future. It helps the other person understand that their words or actions had a negative impact on you, regardless of whether they hurt you. This potentially awkward interaction adds to our own growth and development.

Sadly, many of us see asking questions as a sign of *weakness* ("I really don't know much"), not strength ("I want to learn so that my words and actions don't hurt someone in the future"). We've been programmed to think that asking too many questions might suggest that we're unintelligent or uninformed. Many of us would rather stay quiet in social situations and pretend we understand something than ask for the help we need.

If you are really trying to "college" in the most meaningful way, *ask questions* as frequently as you can (refer back to chapter 1 for an explanation of the explorer's mind-set). The more you ask for clarification, the more informed you will be.

***

Part I of this book focused on how your identity will shift and grow as you transition from high school to college and how you should best interact with your roommate(s), other students on campus, and your residence hall staff. Part II will move the discussion into the heart of your collegiate experience: the college classroom. You'll learn about the expectations that apply to college-level work and how to demonstrate professionalism in your academics; get tools and tips to help you study, write, and participate successfully; and learn about the resources your college will offer to support you in your studies.

PART II

COLLEGE IS SCHOOL

Look around you. The sophomores, juniors, and seniors on campus were all first-year students once. They had the same questions as you and made the same mistakes you're going to make (you will make mistakes in every new situation; that's not only normal, it's something your professors and employers expect and plan for).

Although most college graduates will tell you that they learned as much outside the classroom as in it, at the end of the day, college is still school. The first day of college classes is a part of the "back to school" feeling that you will hopefully find familiar.

With that said, if you're feeling anxious about this brand-new back-to-school experience, you're not alone. After years of sharing our students' first days of college, we understand and expect that they'll have mixed emotions, such as:

- Excitement to take the classes they chose and work toward the careers they hope to pursue.

- Exhilaration about the social opportunities, personal freedom, new friends, and endless supply of on- and off-campus activities that are competing with academics for their attention.

- Anxiety about how they will measure up to their peers and whether they'll meet their professors' expectations (see chapter 1 to learn about imposter syndrome and for strategies to address these concerns).
- Uncertainty about how to manage their workload and prepare for their first midterm exams and papers.
- Confusion about the expectations they're supposed to meet.

If any of these feelings sounds familiar to you, don't worry—you're in the same place as millions of successful students who came before you. In this section, we'll help you get ready for college academics.

In chapter 4, we'll explain how college is different from high school; the mysteries of "critical thinking" and higher-order reasoning; and what professors expect from you, including professionalism, standards for writing and argument, class participation, academic integrity, and information literacy.

In chapters 5 through 8, we will provide tools to help you succeed in (and even enjoy) your college classes.

You'll try out some of our time-tested strategies—such as going to office hours and working with your research librarians—after you get to school. But if you're reading this book before you go, you absolutely *can* give some of them a try. For example, you can find, read, and take notes on an academic journal article; download your syllabi (often available a week before classes start or by request from your professor) and familiarize yourself with each course's requirements; select a calendar and begin to populate it with important dates; write a professional email to your professor; and discuss and develop your personal goals for writing and class participation.

We recommend that you read this section again when classes start, create your assessment calendar, and use the strategies for your college work.

4

WHAT DO YOU WANT FROM ME?
ACADEMIC STANDARDS

While there was less overall physical work than I had in high school, there was way more mental work involved in the assignments I had for almost every class I had. I also wasn't prepared for how succinct I had to be in papers, something I'm very much still working on, going into my fifth semester.

—COLLEGE STUDENT

You've been working hard in school for over a decade and have shown you can succeed at the high school level. That's something to be proud of and will form a good foundation for the next step.

We have found that there's a big difference between college work and what our students have been doing to date. We also know that once we explain college-level expectations to our students, they thrive. But for some reason, no one seems to be *telling* them what to expect and how to succeed. So that's what we'll do here.

In this chapter, we'll take some of the mystery out of college academics, including the differences between high school and college, higher-order ("critical") thinking, standards for writing, and academic integrity.

ADJUSTING TO COLLEGE SCHEDULES AND RESPONSIBILITIES

At this point, you've probably noticed a common theme about the differences between high school and college: you are now in the driver's seat. Your family is supporting you and cheering you on, but not participating in your academic life. Your professors will expect you to take the initiative to seek help and meet your goals.

This means that you need to be your own supervisor. In chapter 5, we'll offer strategies for managing your assignments across a semester and building successful relationships with your professors. But in the meantime, you can consider your work habits and get honest feedback from your family about how much you relied on them or your teachers to keep you on track.

DISCUSS BEFORE YOU GO

- How often did your parents or family members remind you to do your homework, start working on a paper, or study for a test?
- Did you do the required readings, or rely on class lectures to learn the material?
- When you were having a hard time in a class, did you approach the teacher early, wait until you earned a disappointing grade, or did the teacher come to you?

ADJUSTING TO COLLEGE ACADEMIC STANDARDS

In college you will be asked to engage with texts and concepts in more sophisticated ways than before. You will move beyond demonstrating that you *comprehend* the ideas you are studying: you will write persuasive original arguments about them; be challenged to consider both sides of an issue; compare and critique texts about a common topic; and hone your research methods to evaluate the sources you use to support your arguments.

	HIGH SCHOOL	COLLEGE
TIME MANAGEMENT	All students' school days begin and end at the same time each weekday.	Your classes will most likely meet between once and three times per week, and your schedule will vary from day to day.
PROFESSIONALISM AND PERSONAL RESPONSIBILITY	Your parents might be in contact with your teachers, and a teacher or the principal reaches out to them if there is a problem.	You are responsible for contacting professors or seeking academic resources if you need help or have concerns.
	Your teachers remind you when your work is due.	You will be responsible for keeping up with your work.
	You have many homework assignments that give you a sense of how you're doing early in the year.	Your midterm exam or first paper one month into the course might be the first time you get feedback about your progress and comprehension of the subject matter (unless you talk to your professor).
PREPARATION FOR CLASS	Your teachers will often explain the readings and relevant concepts in class.	You will be expected to understand most of what you read before class begins, and the professors will build from there in their lecture or a class discussion.

	HIGH SCHOOL	COLLEGE
ANALYSIS	Demonstrating that you understand the readings is often sufficient to earn a good grade.	Comprehension is only the beginning; you will compare, analyze, and evaluate the texts you read and generate new ideas that apply what you know.
WRITING	Most of your writing will be "expository"—it explains what you know.	Most of your writing will be "persuasive"—you will make original claims and provide evidence to prove your points.
RESEARCH	Most of your work will not involve original research that requires you to curate and evaluate sources of evidence.	As college progresses, more original research will be required, and you will be required to demonstrate that you understand which sources are credible and relevant.
READING	Most of your readings will be textbooks designed for your year in high school.	You will be assigned journal articles and books written by and for experts in the field, information from government sources (such as statistics about school dropout rates for an education course, or budget data for a business course), and historical documents, among others. There will also be more reading, and because you will likely have fewer graded assessments (quizzes, papers, exams), each will cover more course readings—which means you must take notes to retain your knowledge over a longer period.
ACADEMIC INTEGRITY	Teachers might handle issues such as plagiarism or cheating with you and your parents.	Your school's academic integrity code or honor code will likely impose heavy penalties.

UNPACKING THE MYSTERIES OF HIGHER-ORDER ("CRITICAL") THINKING

If you had a nickel for every time someone told you to use "critical thinking," you wouldn't need to take out student loans. And if you had a nickel for every time someone told you what critical thinking *actually means*, you probably wouldn't be able to do a load of laundry.

At a basic level, *critical thinking* means objective analysis and evaluation of an issue or text. Your college courses will require you to comprehend complex ideas; analyze, compare, and evaluate texts and concepts; and craft arguments in which you make objective claims you support with credible, relevant sources.

WHEN YOU'RE THERE

More often than not, when one of our first-year students earns a very low grade on a paper, it is because they didn't fulfill the requirements of the assignment. Read assignment prompts thoroughly. If you have a question about what the professor expects, ask (more than 24 hours before the assignment is due).

Analyzing and Evaluating Ideas and Sources

Excellent college-level work also demonstrates what we call higher-order thinking. Demonstrating that you have learned and understand the material is a large part of high school work. Often, high school teachers spend class time explaining assigned readings and helping students with their knowledge and comprehension.

In most college courses, the professor will expect you to recall the facts and understand the ideas explained in your course readings before you arrive in class. Class discussions will require you to work in the higher levels of thinking—applying, analyzing, comparing, and evaluating texts and ideas.

As you progress through your education, you will be expected to do the following in your papers and class discussions.

- Apply rules and concepts to solve problems
- Identify trends, patterns, and inconsistencies
- Combine existing ideas and theories to create new ones
- Compare theories, texts, ideas, or systems
- Evaluate, judge, or assess ideas
- Recommend original solutions or answers

Here are examples of engagement with an idea from one of the authors' college courses, an introduction to constitutional law. The topic is the First Amendment right to freedom of speech. The assigned reading was a Supreme Court opinion about burning the US flag (*Texas v. Johnson*).

Knowledge (recall of facts)	**Mr. Johnson was arrested for burning a US flag outside the 1984 Republican National Convention and convicted under a Texas law banning flag desecration.**
Comprehension (understanding and summarizing ideas)	**The Supreme Court ruled that burning the flag is speech and the Texas law violated the First Amendment. The Court said Texas couldn't punish people for speech simply because it offends and upsets others.**
	The Court said that the ban on flag burning was not like a law that made it a crime to burn a draft card. Flag burning only offends people, but burning a draft card interferes with the military's work.
Application (using problem-solving methods)	**Asking a question: If a state passed a law punishing student athletes for "taking a knee" during the national anthem, would the *Texas v. Johnson* decision apply there, too?**
	Answering that question: Taking a knee is similar to/different from burning a flag because . . .

Analysis (recognizing trends and patterns)	Asking a question/making an observation: It seems like the Supreme Court doesn't consider emotional harm to be a valid reason to punish someone; would the draft card case come out differently today, when all information about who was eligible for the draft would be available online?
Synthesis (inferring, predicting, and combining)	I predict that the Supreme Court would strike down a law that punishes college athletes for taking a knee during the national anthem because it does no harm other than to offend people.
Evaluation—judging, assessing theories.	Responding to the previous comment: I agree that there is no harm to others, but the case is different. Student athletes are receiving an education from the state and have to follow many conditions and rules to play. Johnson was in a public place and wasn't getting any benefits from the government.

ADAPTING TO HIGHER STANDARDS FOR WRITING

College students and professors generally agree that the transition from high school to college writing is significant.

What's with that, anyway? You've been writing essays for over a decade, from "what I did last summer" in fourth grade to your AP English essay about *The Odyssey*. So why is college any different?

In some ways, it's the same—you need to fulfill the requirements of the assignment, demonstrate that you understand the material, and turn in a polished product on time.

MOVING FROM EXPLAINING TO PERSUADING

In your college writing seminars, you might hear the terms *expository* and *persuasive* writing. Expository writing simply explains a concept or set of facts. Newspaper articles reporting an event (for example, an update on the youth soccer team and their coach who were trapped in a cave in Thailand) are expository. Persuasive writing makes an argument (for example, arguing that youth sports programs help at-risk students improve their academic performance and avoid disciplinary problems, and supporting the argument with credible evidence).

Most college papers will be persuasive pieces—you will craft arguments, not just explanations. The goal of a college paper is to persuade the reader that your claims are true.

> **When writing an essay that requires research, make sure to look into the validity of your sources . . . make sure to understand who wrote the piece you are citing, why they wrote it, and the source's accuracy. In high school, just about any source that sounded good would suffice—that is not the case in college.**
>
> **—COLLEGE STUDENT**

Making Objective (Provable) Claims

Persuasive writing includes opinion writing—such as a newspaper column or blog from an individual's perspective—and objective or scholarly writing. In most cases, your college assignments will require you to state and prove an objective claim—not state a personal (subjective) opinion. You can recognize an objective claim because it is provable. A subjective opinion is not.

Whether you are speaking in class, writing a paper, or answering an exam question, you are going to need to make—and prove—objective claims.

OBJECTIVE (PROVABLE) CLAIMS	SUBJECTIVE (NOT PROVABLE) OPINIONS
The campus meal plan features vegetarian and gluten-free meal options.	The campus meal plan is great.
Governor Jackson has sided with big banks 90 percent of the time.	Governor Jackson is immoral.

Supporting Claims with Credible Evidence

When writing a college paper, you must support every claim you make with evidence. Not all sources of information are evidence; only credible, objective, relevant sources can support your arguments. In college, you'll learn and apply the standards we use to evaluate sources. We call this skill "information literacy." The basics are:

- **UNDERSTANDING THE DIFFERENCE BETWEEN OPINION PIECES AND FACTUAL OR SCHOLARLY PIECES.** An op-ed by a US senator can show you an interesting perspective, but her statement "We need universal healthcare now" is a claim, not evidence to support one.

- **RECOGNIZING ISSUES THAT COULD UNDERMINE YOUR SOURCE'S CREDIBILITY.** For example, if the author's research about the impact of petroleum use on climate change was paid for by a company that produces electric cars, you might think she could be biased. If the author you are quoting, even though he is at a reputable university, has repeatedly been criticized for mischaracterizing his research results or has been forced to retract one or more publications, you might conclude that he is not credible.

- **USING ONLY SOURCES THAT ARE RELEVANT TO YOUR CLAIMS.** For example, a study about the impact of free public transportation vouchers on student performance in Chicago might not be relevant to a paper about rural schools. Older sources might also be less relevant than new ones, especially if some significant event has happened since the source was written.

Putting It All Together

MYTH VS. FACT

MYTH: Every professor wants something different.

FACT: Although professors might have different priorities and approaches, successful college writing has some common features.

No book can tell you how to ace every college class—if we could write a book like that, we would! Unlike your high school classes, college courses don't necessarily follow a standardized curriculum. Professor Jensen's section of Sociology 101 could have different readings and assignments than Professor Fujii's section. And those two professors could grade somewhat differently. For example, Professor Fujii could be somewhat forgiving about grammatical errors, but require students to present sophisticated arguments. Professor Jensen might heavily mark down sloppy papers but not demand as much originality.

This leads to one of the biggest myths in college: "Every professor wants something different." Fortunately, that's not the whole story. The fact is, although professors might prioritize the elements of a good paper differently, most of them agree about what constitutes successful college work.

Every professor wants you to:

- Fulfill every requirement in the assignment.

- Demonstrate that you understand the material.

- Make a provable claim and support it with objective evidence (unless you've been asked to write an op-ed or personal narrative).

- State your thesis and briefly summarize your argument at the beginning of your paper. Suspense makes for a great screenplay, but it kills an academic paper. Explicitly inform your readers what you plan to prove (your thesis) in the very first paragraph.

- Write a logical argument that a reader can follow and understand.

- Turn in something that looks like you worked hard on it and wrote a second draft.

- Honor the page limit (though some will care about this more than others).

No professor wants you to:
- Waste half your paper restating the question.

- Leave them wondering what your paper is about, only to reveal your point in the final paragraph.

- Turn in something sloppy.

- Make unsupported claims.

- Use flawed sources—such as a conspiracy theory website.

Standards for style and format may vary by academic discipline. For example, legal writing usually includes numbered sections and subsections. By contrast, these are not commonly used in marketing papers. Ask your professors if they have model papers or examples of writing in their discipline.

WHEN YOU'RE THERE

Read your professors' written feedback on your papers. That is a road map for improving your writing and your grades. If your professor doesn't provide feedback or you want to know more, go to their office hours and ask what you can do to take your writing to the next level.

PARTICIPATING IN CLASS

PRO-TIP

Even if your professor doesn't grade class participation, it's important to engage meaningfully in class discussions. Participating in class helps you learn and recall the material better, which will help you succeed in the course.

Many first-year students are anxious about speaking up in class. This is particularly true for students who:

- Consider themselves shy.

- Are worried they know less than their peers (see "imposter syndrome" in chapter 1).

- Hold views their classmates don't share.

- Are not native English speakers or have an accent that's not common in their student body.

- Have a speech-related disability.

It's understandable to be worried about speaking up in a room full of other smart people or in front of a professor who's an expert in their field. But once you know what successful class participation is about, you'll be more confident that you can contribute meaningfully to discussions—and be recognized for it.

> **If you're scared to participate, commit to saying one thing per class period. It's scary at first, but with practice, it gets easier.**
> —COLLEGE STUDENT

What Are They Looking For, Anyway?

PRO-TIP

Your professors can tell when you haven't done the reading.

PREPARATION

Do the reading. Your professor will not walk into the room and explain the readings; she will typically ask a question about the reading and then lead a conversation about it. Class participation demonstrates that you have done the reading.

If you have read the assigned reading but don't understand it, you can ask a question (or, if called on, explain what confused you about the text). (See chapter 6 for strategies for successful reading and how to read a journal article.)

ENGAGEMENT WITH THE QUESTION PRESENTED

Professors design their class discussions and questions with specific learning goals in mind. Most want to lead a conversation. Class participation isn't about making speeches; it's about contributing to a discussion with the group. The class discussion will be about course concepts—not a time to rehash what you learned in a high school course or club.

Do:

- Listen carefully to your professor's question.
- Answer the question presented.
- Relate your answer to the assigned readings.

Don't:

- Simply say what you had planned to say when you arrived in class, regardless of whether it's responsive to the question.

- Say, "That's not the most important question—the *real* question is . . ." Your professor asked *that* question for a reason. Stating that it's unimportant is disrespectful to your professor and shows that you might not want to work toward the lesson's objectives.

- Talk about your own opinions without regard to what the professor has asked.

ENGAGING IN CONVERSATION WITH YOUR PEERS

Class discussions are designed to get students engaging not only with course materials, but with one another. You can learn a lot from your peers, but to do so, you have to listen. A successful class isn't about individual students taking turns making speeches; it's a respectful conversation.

Do:

- Listen carefully to what your classmates are saying.

- Listen to understand, not only to rebut.

- Respond to and build upon the most recent comment or question.

- Engage with or debate the ideas presented.

- Support your own claims with credible evidence.

Don't:

- Ignore other students' contributions.

- Criticize your classmate(s).

- Respond with a personal opinion.

Contributing to the Learning Community

Being a great classmate is like being a thoughtful gift giver. Remember when you were five and you wanted to give your mom some Legos for Mother's Day? That wouldn't have been a great gift because it wasn't focused on her.

Like giving a thoughtful gift, contributing to the learning community is about the people around you. In deciding what to offer in a class discussion, think about whether it will be productive and useful to others.

This doesn't mean you have to be a mini professor and teach your classmates. A thoughtful question can help the learning process just as much as an answer.

Preparation is essential for successful class participation. In chapter 6, you will learn to prepare for class by reading effectively and taking good notes on what you read. In the meantime, you can prepare by looking at your past performance in the classroom in high school.

DO BEFORE YOU GO

- Reflect on the kind of participant you've been in high school class discussions.

- Think about the feedback you've received about participation. Have you been asked to speak up more? Have classmates or teachers asked you to be more open to different points of view or give others room to speak?

- Set a goal for your college class participation and use the reading and note-taking tips in chapter 6 to help prepare.

WHEN YOU'RE THERE

TALK TO YOUR PROFESSOR. Professors are aware that many students find class participation challenging. Go to your professor to discuss your concerns—particularly if you feel that language barriers or a disability will make class participation more challenging for you. If you have classroom accommodations for a disability, make sure your professor understands them.

FOLLOWING ACADEMIC RULES

Although your high school most likely took academic integrity violations seriously, the stakes are certainly higher in college. Integrity is the foundation of the academic experience on college campuses, and something you will need to understand as soon as possible so that you are ready when classes begin.

Academic integrity is the moral code that builds trust between scholars. Everyone in the academic community, including teachers, researchers, and students, must commit to being truthful and respecting others' work. Without a code, an academic community cannot flourish to its fullest. Assigned grades show if and how students meet the prescribed learning goals. Thus, all work for which students receive grades should result from the student's own efforts.

Why Does Academic Integrity Matter?

- **FAIRNESS:** When a violation goes unreported, the student benefits from their own unethical behavior.

- **VALUE OF THE DEGREE:** Dishonest students devalue the grade and degree other students earn because they have not demonstrated the same skills and knowledge but can claim the same credentials.

- **HONESTY:** Cheating, as well as ignoring the dishonest behavior of other students, fosters a culture of ignoring unethical behavior.

What Are Academic Integrity Violations?

Sometimes academic integrity is violated deliberately in order to attain an unfair advantage. But there are honest mistakes and misunderstandings, especially among first-year students, that are still considered violations of academic integrity. Lots of first-year students are surprised to read what constitutes an academic integrity or honor code violation. Consider the following examples of common academic integrity code violations among students in US colleges and universities:

- Plagiarizing, including copying something from the internet without acknowledgment.

- Cheating on homework, tests, exams, or problem sets.
- Helping other students cheat.
- Failing to report others who cheat.
- Submitting work you completed for one course to meet requirements in another course without prior permission from your professor.
- Inappropriate collaboration on an assignment or test.
- Signing someone else's name on an attendance sheet.
- Receiving information about a test from someone who took it previously.
- Making false claims in order to take a test at a different time.
- Intimidating someone to prevent them from reporting an academic violation.
- Fabricating data.

What Is a College Honor Code or Honor Pledge?

Many (but not all) schools have an honor code to which students must adhere. On many campuses, students will be asked to affirm their awareness of the school honor code when they matriculate. Some schools ask students to sign an honor pledge as a group during orientation and/or when they take tests and exams. The honor code or pledge shows that students have committed to the integrity of their academic work.

What Happens When Students Violate the Academic Integrity Code or Honor Code?

There are consequences for breaking a college's academic integrity or honor code, but the university body that oversees the code-violation hearing differs from school to school. Every college handles these violations differently, ranging from a written warning to failure on an assignment to failure in a class to dismissal from the university.

★★★

Hopefully, this chapter took some of the mystery out of college academics. Now that you have a basic sense of *what* professors will expect from you, you're ready to learn *how* to meet those expectations. Professionalism is the first and most important college academic skill. It's adulting for academics. In chapter 5, you'll learn some skills and habits characteristic of successful college students—and successful adults.

5

GOING PRO: PROFESSIONALISM IN COLLEGE ACADEMICS

In college, many things that you might have previously felt should only happen if you're struggling are instead behaviors practiced by the most successful students. That includes visiting professors to chat one-on-one, emailing them for feedback on drafts and other work, asking lots of questions, admitting what you're not sure about or don't know, and otherwise putting yourself out there and being in contact with professors (and all the other resources available to you). The more you do these things, the better you'll do, and the more successful and meaningful your college experience will be!

—COLLEGE PROFESSOR

Hopefully reading chapter 4 took some of the mystery out of college work (however, the ingredients of some campus dining hall offerings will probably remain mysteries for all time). But how do you put goals into practice?

In this chapter, you'll learn about adulting for academics, which we call professionalism. The most successful students approach college academics as if every class were a job. Think about the things that would get you in trouble at a job (or even get you fired):

- Frequent lateness
- Not completing tasks on time
- Being disrespectful of coworkers, your boss, or your customers
- Depending upon others to complete your own responsibilities

When I came into college I thought that since I had more free time, I would be able to get my work done faster and be able to prioritize. However, with all the free time, I kept telling myself, "You can do it later," until it was too late and I would stress out. What I do now is I have a whiteboard where I put everything I need to do for the day, and I plan out what time I will do each thing, so that I can get all of my work done and still have free time to relax or be social.

—COLLEGE STUDENT

You might notice a common thread here: before people even see how well you perform a task, you need to show them you're doing it when it's needed and required. The time management section will help you set yourself up to succeed in this goal.

In college courses, punctuality and reliability are just as important as they are at a job. Even though you have a great deal of freedom to decide how to spend your time, you need to treat your class meetings as if they were shifts at your job or internship. Be there. Be on time. Be ready. Be presentable.

This not only includes class attendance (even if your professor doesn't take attendance), but also completing your written assignments on time and preparing adequately for quizzes, presentations, and exams.

A first-year student showed she was mature and responsible from the first day of class. She was always on time; used clear, respectful emails when she had a question; listened thoughtfully; did the reading daily; and turned in her assignments on time. By the time final exams came around, I knew her to be a competent, responsible, engaged student. Unfortunately, a very serious issue with her roommate caused her not to get any sleep the night before the final exam, which was scheduled for 8:10 a.m. She came to the exam on time and said that she would take it if she had to but asked whether there was any way she could have some time to sleep first. I granted her request. It was an easy call, because I knew she was responsible and had done her part to prepare.

—COLLEGE PROFESSOR

In chapter 9, you'll explore strategies for managing your time in a way that supports your well-being—finding time to eat, sleep, exercise, socialize, participate in activities that bring you joy, and complete your classwork. You'll complete a "168 exercise" that shows you how to budget your time in any given week.

To responsibly prepare for your college course load, you'll also need to take the long view. There will be some weeks when writing a paper or studying for a midterm occupies most of your academic time. Other weeks might be more balanced. Because your professors design their courses independently, you might have papers due and exams on the same day. It's helpful to plan ahead and create a calendar that lays out your whole semester. You can do this by: (1) selecting a master calendar system, which you should do over the summer; and (2) creating an "assessment calendar" that shows the dates of every graded exercise—quizzes, papers, presentations, and exams.

DO BEFORE YOU GO

Choose a Calendar and Start Using It

- Choose a calendar format that you can find and edit easily and that you will be able to print and display in your room. Suggestions:
  - A Google doc or similar electronic document you can bookmark in your computer and phone browsers
  - The calendar function from your personal or school email account
  - A document that you save to your computer's desktop or home screen
  - A paper planner, if you've had success using one before (get one that provides lots of room for scheduling each day)
  - Your phone's calendar
- Find your school's academic calendar for your first semester. Save a copy on your computer, print it out, and bookmark the link on your smartphone, or if you can, link the calendar to your phone's calendar.
- Start populating your calendar with dates from the school's academic calendar, including the first and last days of classes, exam study period, and any days off (such as Labor Day).
- If you have time and your syllabi are available online, you might start creating an academic assessment calendar (see p. 76). Otherwise, mark your master calendar with a reminder to work on your assessment calendar.
- If you will be observing any religious holidays that conflict with class meetings, make a note to email your professors as soon as possible. (See chapter 9 for information about religious accommodations.)

How to Create an Assessment Calendar

Your assessment calendar gives you a heads-up about when your work is due and enables you to plan ahead. Here is an example of a one-month chunk of an assessment calendar. In this case, the student put the assignments for each of her classes in a different format. You could also color-code them.

November						
SUN	MON	TUES	WED	THUR	FRI	SAT
		1 Stats midterm	2	3 Journalism Op-ed 25%	4	5
6	7	8 Psych quiz	9	10	11 History midterm 30%	12
13	14	15 Stats quiz	16	17	18	19
20	21 Journalism quiz	22 Psych quiz	23	24	25 Thanksgiving break	26
27	28	29	30	1	2	

How to Make Your Assessment Calendar:

1. Check your school email and online academic portal for course syllabi. Most professors will post their syllabi at least a week before classes.

2. Review all syllabi and find the following:

   a. Descriptions of the assessments (graded assignments) that will make up your final grade. Here's an example from a syllabus:

Class participation:	10%
Written reflections:	10%
First paper:	25%
Group project:	20%
Final paper:	35%

   b. The dates for all graded assessments: quizzes, papers, midterms, exams, presentations, and other assignments.

3. Insert every graded assessment into the calendar. You might choose to label each course with a different color and/or note when the assignment is a large part of your course grade.

4. Print your calendar and post it by your bed or desk; keep another copy in your organizer or backpack.

5. If you use a paper organizer, build your assessment calendar in it.

It's very tempting to procrastinate in college when you don't have any parents around reminding you what to do. Keep a planner handy and write everything down. Trust me, it is possible to get all your assignments done, relax, spend time with friends, join clubs, and even have a job.

—COLLEGE STUDENT

COMMUNICATING LIKE A PROFESSIONAL

College professors frequently complain that their first-year students don't know how to communicate like professionals. A large part of the problem is that their students don't know how to follow the conventions of email etiquette. That makes sense, because most high school students have not been taught how.

When you communicate with professors, you need to follow the unwritten rules of professional communication.

Some professors will explicitly tell you that they need 24 to 48 hours to respond to an email, excluding weekends. Even if they don't, it's safe to assume that this is their policy and to act accordingly. Do not send a follow-up request for a response for at least two days, excluding weekends, after your initial email.

Writing a Professional Email

Learning to write a professional email is a crucial skill to hone before college, and one you can take with you into the world outside your campus. A courteous and thoughtfully constructed request is much more likely to receive the kind of response you want.

You will frequently email your college professors, TAs, and other college staff members once you're on campus. Now's the time to learn how to do it.

Make sure to use your assigned college email address, not a personal one. Here's a template you can follow in constructing an email to a professor, supervisor, or college staff member. Each element is explained further below.

Salutation [person's title] [last name],
Introductory line that recognizes something pleasant.
Reminder of how they know you.
The real reason for your email.

Polite restatement of your request.

Sign-off,

Your name

SALUTATION

Use "Dear" or "Hello" to establish the relationship.

PERSON'S TITLE

Use the person's proper title to communicate respect for their position. If you are unsure, look up their professional title online. "Professor" is the most appropriate title for any college faculty member. If you are sending a professional email to someone on campus who is not a professor, make sure you are using the correct title, such as "Director," "Dr.," "Dean," or "Assistant Provost." If you cannot find their title, use "Mr." or "Ms." It is never appropriate to use "Miss," "Mrs.," or a first name unless you have been given explicit permission to do so.

LAST NAME

Make sure to spell the person's last name correctly. If there is a hyphen in it, or if it is a two-part last name, use the hyphen and/or both names.

INTRODUCTORY LINE THAT RECOGNIZES
SOMETHING PLEASANT

A thoughtful sentence such as, "I hope you're enjoying the weather today," or "I hope you had a relaxing weekend," acknowledges that the person you are emailing has a life outside their job on campus. The ritual politeness of an introductory sentence (similar to a "How are you?" in spoken conversation) is expected in professional emails.

REMINDER OF HOW THEY KNOW YOU

This is particularly important, especially if it's the first time you are contacting this person. You can't count on them to remember your name from their rosters or to be able to put your face with your name. "I'm in your [section number and class name] that meets on [day of the week] at [time]" will help clarify who you are from perhaps hundreds of their students in a given semester. They might also be getting a similar question or request from multiple students. If there's something distinctive about you that would jog their memory and make them look upon you fondly, such as, "I stayed after class to ask you about the reading today," include that.

If you haven't met this person yet, explain your desired relationship to them, such as "I am interested in enrolling in your class next semester," "I am hoping to serve as a Peer Educator in your office next semester," or "I would like to set up a meeting with you to talk about my roommate contract."

THE REAL REASON FOR YOUR EMAIL

Think about the reason you are sending the email. Ideally, you will concisely state what you need without going into excessive detail or sounding like you are making excuses or demands. If you can't explain why you're emailing in a sentence or two, consider making an appointment to meet with this person, in which case your email can simply be a request for a meeting.

POLITE RESTATEMENT OF YOUR REQUEST

This is your summary sentence and a nod to a request that you would like them to add to their to-do list. If you need this person to fill out a form, contact someone on your behalf, or help you set up a meeting—something that requires more action than just answering your email—state that very clearly. If you're simply asking a question you need an answer to, you can say something like, "I would appreciate if you could let me know at your earliest convenience."

SIGN-OFF

"Sincerely" is always an appropriate way to end an email, but "Thank you," does double duty as both a sign-off and an expression of gratitude.

YOUR NAME

You should use the name you identify with to introduce yourself and close your email, but if this name is different than the name your professor will find for you on their class roster, it is important that you also let them know this in the closing of your email. If you want to specify which pronouns you use (he/him/his, she/her/hers, they/them/theirs), you could also do so here.

DO BEFORE YOU GO

Send a Professional Email

It's a great idea to try this technique over the summer by emailing your professors to introduce yourself. This is not only a good way to practice before you get too busy, but it will help break the ice and make you more comfortable with your professors when you meet. If you don't have a specific request, that's okay. Introducing yourself is still a great idea.

You could also email an academic adviser, financial aid counselor, residence life staff member, or anyone else who has information you need or want to know.

SAMPLE INTRODUCTION EMAIL TO YOUR PROFESSOR:

Dear Professor Yang,

I hope that you are having a good summer.

My name is Tonya Jennings, and I am an incoming first-year student from Des Moines, Iowa. I am enrolled in your Introduction to Philosophy course, PHI 101-003 (Tuesdays and Fridays at 10:30) this semester. I am not sure whether I will major in philosophy yet, but I am excited to take this class.

I hope to introduce myself in your office hours when I arrive on campus.

Sincerely,
Tonya Jennings
Class of 2023

Communicating in Person

When you meet with your professor—whether in office hours, before or after class, or at a study session—come prepared (just as you would for a class or exam). Always bring paper and a pen to take notes. State your question or concern clearly.

Do:

- Come on time to any scheduled meetings.
- Bring paper and a pen for notes.
- Bring the assignment or reading about which you have a question.
- If you have a form for them to sign, print it yourself and bring it.

Don't:

- Eat or drink during the meeting without asking first.
- Take notes on your phone (it looks like you're not paying attention, and also doesn't give you room to write extensive notes).
- Stop by unannounced outside office hours.

STAYING PROFESSIONAL WHILE USING TECHNOLOGY

PRO-TIP

Check out your course syllabi when you get them. Do the classes require you to use specialized computer programs or research tools? If so, check the library website for resources to help you get familiar with them.

You have grown up using technology. From smartphones to Google searches, you integrate technology into your personal and academic life more seamlessly than anyone. You can improve your academic performance by using technology wisely and independently. You can also frustrate professors and miss deadlines by using it poorly. Here are some technology dos and don'ts for your academic career.

Do:

- Learn to use the online portal that your school uses for courses. Your professor is likely to post the course syllabus, supplemental readings, and announcements there.
- Bookmark the technology support website on your browser and program their contact information into your smartphone.

- Make use of proofreading and antiplagiarism programs for papers and assignments.
- Check your university email daily.

Don't:

- Reach out to your professor through social media or professional networking websites.
- Ask your professor to serve as tech support. It is up to you to submit your assignments on time—including through systems like Blackboard, MyEdu, and Canvas.
- Rely solely on proofreading programs, which don't always catch mistakes such as misuse of *their, they're,* and *there.*

DO BEFORE YOU GO

- Install the online course portal app on your smartphone.
- Connect your school email account to your smartphone.
- Consider installing a shared document app such as Google Docs. That way if you save your course syllabi as online documents, you'll always be able to view them on your phone.

***

Your habits as a student—being on time, showing respect for your professors' time and position, communicating clearly and appropriately, and using technology independently and properly—will serve you in college and in life. Remember to maintain your professionalism even when you are tired and stressed. If and when you are having a tough time, you'll be glad you demonstrated that you're professional and responsible from the beginning. Being prepared for every class is essential to demonstrating that you take your education seriously. Next, you'll learn strategies for class preparation, reading, and studying.

6

GET TO THE POINT:
READ AND STUDY WITH PURPOSE

At the beginning of the semester, you will look at the syllabus and see that all the major papers are due in November, and you will say, "I'm fine, I have plenty of time." Do not fall into that trap. Before you know it, November will be upon you and all the papers will be due in the same week. Space out your assignments according to class so you have equal time for all of them.

—COLLEGE STUDENT

As you learned in chapter 4, you will be responsible for understanding your course readings before every class. Here you'll learn some strategies successful students use when reading and preparing for class. You'll also get some tips about successful habits for college exams and quizzes (and reviewing your class readings to prepare to write papers).

READING FOR CLASS

FAST FACT

Many professors assign reading for the first class. Read the syllabus as soon as it's available and make time to read before classes start. Your professor could call on you on the very first day.

First, you need to make sure you can do the reading. At the beginning of each week, check the syllabus and emails from professors. Make sure you have access to the readings. Are they in your textbook? On the online course portal? On reserve in the library? It's your responsibility to get access to whatever is assigned. Also check how long the readings are and adjust your study schedule accordingly.

A very important thing to note: When professors assign you a reading, do it. So many professors draw their lesson from the readings, and they *will* call you out.

—COLLEGE STUDENT

Take Notes on Your Readings— But Don't Rewrite Them

Studies have shown that taking notes (by hand) helps students comprehend what they read. But how? And how much is too much? Our students sometimes tell us that they are having a hard time completing their readings because it takes them so long to take notes. Here are some strategies for effective note taking:

1. Read an entire section of an article or chapter before writing extensive notes. You want to take in a full concept and its explanation before interrupting yourself to write. After that, write down the main point.

2. Don't underline or highlight everything in the book, especially as you read. You won't know the most important points until you finish.

3. Sticky notes are a great way to mark the spots that seem important or items you'd like to review without interrupting the flow of your reading (they're also helpful if you've rented or plan to sell your books). You can go back and remove them or write a few words on them when you finish reading. They're a great way to make sure you can find a textual source to use in support of any points you make in class or in a written assignment. If you're using the electronic version of a book, you can often use the underline or comment function like a sticky note.

4. After you complete each reading, take a moment to write or type the main idea and plan to bring your notes to class.

5. Write down your questions, not only what you know and understand. Asking questions is a great way to contribute to class discussion, and shows you are thinking hard about what you are studying.

6. Challenge yourself to think deeply about the readings through the "I noticed and I wondered" approach. This is a way to connect what you learn to a broader idea about the material. For example: "I noticed that the psychology experiment in this article didn't mention whether the subjects took medication, and I wondered whether that would make a difference to the results."

One piece of advice I can offer is to not expect answers to be force-fed to you the way they were in high school. I've found that a lot of students get frustrated when there's material on tests that "was never even talked about in class."

—COLLEGE STUDENT

How to Read an Academic Journal Article

First-year students report that one of the most stressful academic challenges they face is learning to read academic journal articles. This type of writing is rarely seen in high school but is frequently assigned as required reading in college. If you can master the tips and tricks to skimming and processing an academic journal article for content before you arrive on campus, your first college homework assignment will be much easier for you to understand . . . and *that* will reduce your stress!

Academic journal articles (also referred to as scholarly journal articles or peer-reviewed articles) are published in almost every academic field. Academic journal articles can take many forms: they can present original research, clinical case studies, or trials; provide critical analysis of existing work in the field; review concepts, prevalent ideas, and theories; or offer reviews of books.

Whatever form they take, you can guarantee that scholarly journal articles are credible and authoritative sources of knowledge in a particular academic field. Scholarly journal articles have been reviewed by other faculty members somewhere in the world (hence the term *peer-reviewed*) and edited before publication. In college, you will be assigned journal articles written by your professors and others that display mastery of a particular subject in the field you are studying.

Every once in a while, you will be expected to read through the entire study assigned to you. However, most of the time, you will need to read just enough to understand the gist of the study or report on the major findings of the author(s). Therefore, learning the proper way to skim and process this highly specialized information will be invaluable to you over the next four years. Since there is often a lot of data presented in an article, it is easy to miss out on essential information—but this can be avoided with preparation and practicing the following six easy steps.

1. **READ THE TITLE OF THE ARTICLE,** which should explain the theme and the key academic language important to a basic understanding of the research. *Take a few notes on what you can decipher about the article based on its title.*

2. **READ THE ABSTRACT,** which is a short, tight outline of the journal article. The abstract presents a summary of the research, explains the importance of the article to the academic field, and offers evidence of the findings and the study conclusion. *Take a few notes on what you have learned about the article based on the abstract.*

3. **READ THE INTRODUCTION,** which includes the topic, thesis or research questions, argument, and theoretical framework. *Take a few notes on what you now understand about the article based on the introduction.*

4. **READ THE REMAINING SECTION HEADINGS AND ANY VISUALS PRESENTED** (such as detailed images, graphs, or charts). *At this point, list all the headings and briefly explain the visuals.*

5. **READ THE CONCLUSION,** which summarizes findings and explains why the issues presented are relevant and important. *Take a few notes on what the journal article concludes.*

6. **REREAD THE NOTES YOU TOOK ON THE FIRST FIVE POINTS.** Rereading your notes will help you process what you have learned. If something in your notes is confusing to you, go back to that particular section and read it slowly and more in-depth.

DO BEFORE YOU GO

The summer before college is a great time to learn how to skim and process an academic journal article so that you will know the best way to approach it when your first one is assigned for college homework.

First, select a journal article unfamiliar to you that you find online—you can use an academic search engine or simply Google an article. Ideally, find one that seems interesting to you and is fewer than ten pages. (Once you are in college, you should think about *why* your professor assigned the article to you. Ask yourself *what* they want you to understand or question.)

Once you have the article selected, follow the six steps for skimming a journal article.

BUILDING EFFECTIVE STUDY HABITS AND STRATEGIES

The fact that you're in college means you've studied before. You've taken tests and quizzes in your classes, you've written essays and papers, and you most likely took one or more standardized tests, such as the SAT, ACT, or AP subject matter tests. College presents new challenges, however. Your living arrangements, workload, and schedule are different. And no one is telling you to study—it's on you.

The most important thing to know about studying in college is that you should be working at a consistent pace, keeping up with your reading for every class rather than cramming before a test or when preparing to write a paper. Students who read effectively and consistently don't need all-nighters to succeed because they are only *reviewing* material for a test—not learning it for the first time.

Get the Most Out of Your Reading and Study Time

Do not do your homework or studying in your room/bed. It is too tempting to take a nap for an hour and then end up losing six hours to a midday nap. If you have notes to take or work to do, go straight to the library.

—COLLEGE STUDENT

LOCATION MATTERS

As you read in chapter 2, you are going to be sharing your living space. Residence halls can be quite loud and distracting, particularly in the late afternoons and evenings, when most people aren't in classes. Most college students report that they do not study as well in their rooms as they do in the library. Your room has too many distractions: your bed, your TV if you have one, and, most important, your friends. When possible, plan to study in the library.

WHEN YOU'RE THERE

Find one or more ideal study spots. A great study area:

- Is on a safe route to your residence hall, if you'll be studying at night.
- Is comfortable.
- Has few distractions.
- Is near your classrooms, if you plan to study between classes.

Test your study spot: time yourself while you do the reading for one class. Next time you study in your room, time yourself again. How long did it take you to read the same number of pages? How does your recall of the material compare?

Busy people, college students included, often take pride in being able to multitask. The fact is, multitasking might be necessary in some circumstances, but it really doesn't work when you're studying. This is even truer in college than in high school because you have more reading to do and the readings you have will be more complex.

DO BEFORE YOU GO

Practice Reading Without Technology Distractions

Set your phone timer to 30 minutes and put the phone in your pocket or behind you with the notification sounds turned on. Read something challenging until the time is up. Consider your reactions when you heard a text come in or the phone ringing. Was it difficult not to check the text? Did you find yourself distracted from the reading because you wondered who was looking for you? How many pages did you read, and how well do you recall the material? Practice this a few times throughout the summer. See whether turning off your phone ringer helps.

Emails, texts, social media, and other internet material are all really tempting when you're studying. If you're reading or writing on your computer, distractions are just a browser window away. When you study, put your phone away. If you are reading a book, close your laptop or turn it to the side. If you find it hard to stay away from the internet and your phone during several hours of studying, use a timer to separate study time from screen time. Set the timer to 30 minutes and focus throughout that time. When the timer goes off (set it to vibrate if you're in the library), finish the point you are reading and, if you wish, give yourself 5 to 10 minutes to check your email or social media. Then set the timer for another 30 minutes of studying.

READ WITH PURPOSE—KNOW WHAT YOU SHOULD KNOW

If you've ever done your household's grocery shopping, you know that you shop faster and end up getting more of what you actually need if you go with a list. Knowing what you want in advance and checking it off the list makes the errand go faster. Your reading and studying is the same way—you'll get more out of the time you spend reading if you start your reading with a sense of what you're supposed to be learning. Sometimes that's easy: if your reading is in a textbook, the chapter titles and table of contents give you a good sense of what the main points are. However, we have found that sometimes students aren't sure why certain readings were assigned and what they're supposed to be learning. But how do you know what you should know?

WHEN YOU'RE THERE

Tips for Studying with Purpose

- **READ THE SYLLABUS CLOSELY.** Does the syllabus list a topic for the next class (example: "understanding the legislative process" in a government course or "development across the life-span" in a psychology course)? Look for parts of the reading that help you understand that topic better.
- **PAY ATTENTION TO THE TYPES OF QUESTIONS YOUR PROFESSORS ASK IN CLASS.** Do they ask students to recall specific facts and figures? Compare ideas in different readings? Explain the main idea of an article? Tailor your reading and note taking accordingly.
- **TALK TO YOUR PROFESSORS.** Ask them what kinds of questions they will ask on tests and how the course readings relate to each other and to the overall course objectives.
- **WORK WITH CLASSMATES.** Find someone who will discuss the material with you at least once per week. See if you're noticing the same things in the readings and in class.

TAKE BREAKS

We've said it before, and it's true: college is hard, and it's supposed to be. Working constantly isn't the right way to succeed. You have to take breaks—not only to eat, sleep, and look after yourself, but to give your mind a chance to absorb everything you've read. Plan your study time in blocks with significant daily downtime. If you're using your time wisely and not letting distractions extend your daily reading hours, you will be able to rest.

TAKE IT UP A NOTCH FOR TESTS AND EXAMS

If you have been reading consistently, engaging in class discussion, and paying attention to the kinds of questions your professor asks, you have no reason to panic before your first exam. When preparing for a test, apply the same principles you used for your daily reading, but this time, study your own notes. Some professors post their class slide presentations online or will give them to students upon request. If the slides are available, they can be a great study guide.

WHEN YOU'RE THERE

Using your assessment calendar (see chapter 5), plan blocks of time to study for tests and exams. Plan your first big block early enough so that you will have time to visit the professor's office hours if you have questions. Example: If your test is on Friday, October 25, and the professor's office hours are on Tuesdays, make sure you have reviewed all of your reading and class notes before Tuesday the twenty-second.

***

By reading with purpose (and listening with purpose in class), you will learn the material presented in your courses. The next challenge is to demonstrate what you know, and your higher-order thinking skills, by writing coherent, persuasive arguments. In chapter 7, you'll learn techniques for planning, writing, and editing persuasive college papers.

7

THERE ARE NO BAD WRITERS,
ONLY UNPERSUASIVE PAPERS:
COLLEGE WRITING

If you are unsure about the requirements for an assignment or when something is due, ask your professor. This could be in the form of an email, talking to the professor after class, or attending the professor's office hours.

—COLLEGE STUDENT

It's likely that your college will require you to take at least one writing class, possibly in your first semester. Now that you know the standards for college writing, we're going to give you some basic but highly effective strategies for meeting those standards.

A PAPER IS A PERSUASION MACHINE

In chapter 4, you learned that in college you'll be asked to write persuasive papers: you make a claim and then persuade your reader by constructing a logical argument supported by credible evidence. To do that, you need to think of your paper as a machine—not just a stationary object of a certain size.

When judging a car, the most important criterion is whether it gets you from place to place. You would like it to be pretty and have a good sound system and enough cup holders. But you wouldn't say a pretty car body with cool toys in it but no engine was a "good" car. A paper is a machine for persuading your audience. Throughout every stage of your prewriting, writing, and editing, judge your work by whether it's doing its job.

THINK BEFORE YOU WRITE: PREWRITING

A paper has an introduction, body, and conclusion. But when it comes to writing a paper, you don't start with the introduction (in fact, many students write that last). Before you start writing your argument, select and plan it.

During prewriting, follow these steps:

1. Make sure you understand the assignment; if you don't, then check with your professor or TA.

2. Look at your reading notes, class notes, and, if applicable, the results of your independent research, and find the materials that address the question. Jot down some ideas about how to answer the question. If you have time, step away and let them percolate. Get some fresh air, refill your water bottle, or notice a tree.

3. Nail down your one-sentence answer (thesis). Example: "Attempting to survive on the campus meal plan could be dangerous to a student's health."

4. Articulate the points you will make to support your thesis. For example: "(a) The vegetables are prepared in a way that drains vitamins, which can result in vitamin deficiency; (b) there is not enough fiber in the food, which can cause digestion problems; and (c) the food's odors have been proven to cause diners to lose their appetites, which can result in inadequate caloric intake."

5. Put your thesis and supporting points in a document and put spaces between them. Don't start writing sentences and paragraphs. You can use bullets or numbered points. This is the beginning of your outline.

6. Use your reading notes and class notes to identify evidence that will support every one of your claims. Without writing full sentences and paragraphs, put your chunks of evidence between your claims.

7. Now you're ready to start writing the text.

BUILD YOUR MACHINE: WRITING THE FIRST DRAFT

Now it's time to take the parts of your persuasion machine—the outline with evidence—and turn it into something that gets you from point A (the question) to point B (your audience believes your answer). We don't recommend that you focus on making each sentence beautiful, which can interrupt your attempts to prove your points. If you find yourself stumbling over word choice, you can type something like "[**need a word here**]." If you do this, make sure you put it in bold face so that you don't inadvertently leave it there (which you won't do, because you're going to edit, right?).

1. Compare your outline to the assignment prompt. Does your outline have all the elements of a complete answer? Do you refer to as many course texts as required? Is there a missing piece? If something is missing, go back to your prewriting and complete the outline.

2. Fill in your outline by turning each point into a paragraph that states a claim and supports it with evidence.

3. Look over your draft and make sure it looks complete—then take a break (preferably 24 hours).

WHEN YOU'RE THERE

A paragraph contains only one claim plus supporting evidence. If you make more than one claim, you need a new paragraph. Be suspicious of paragraphs that are longer than three or four sentences.

a. Use "signposts" to tell your reader where you are taking them on your road to point B.

Example: "This paper will examine three features of the meal plan and demonstrate that they present measurable threats to human health.

"First, food preparation saps vegetables of vital nutrients."

b. Use transitions to tell your reader how you got from the point before to this one.

Example: "In addition to causing vitamin deficiency, the meal plan also threatens digestion."

c. Answer the question "so what" for every claim and piece of evidence you write.

Example: If you tell your reader that the fiber content is under one gram per meal, tell them why: "An average fiber content of under one gram per meal has been proven to cause digestive tract problems."

WHEN YOU'RE THERE

Much like pizza, a paper draft is even better the next morning (unlike pizza, you don't need to store it in the fridge).

Time your writing process so you can put a break of 12 to 24 hours between your first draft and your editing process.

TEST YOUR MACHINE, TIGHTEN UP THE BOLTS, AND MAKE IT BEAUTIFUL: EDITING

In the editing process, you'll read and adjust your paper three times. Don't worry—if your prewriting process was thorough, this won't be a very tough process.

Make Sure Your Machine Can Get You from Place to Place: First Read-Through

In your first read-through, you'll make sure that your paper does what it was supposed to do (regardless of whether it does so with style and grace).

Here's what to check for during your first read-through:

1. Fulfills the requirements of assignment
2. Contains an explicit, provable thesis at the beginning
3. Contains explicit, provable points to support the thesis
4. Contains evidence to support every claim
5. Organizes points into distinct paragraphs, each of which includes
   1. Claim
   2. Evidence
   3. Transition or signpost

If anything from this checklist is missing, fill it in now before you proceed to the second read-through.

Tightening Your Machine at the Paragraph Level: Second Read-Through

Now you will work on your paragraphs and ensure that each point proceeds logically from the one before.

WHEN YOU'RE THERE

Unsupported claims are paper killers (and grade killers). To check whether you're missing some evidence, print your paper and highlight every claim. If you have two consecutive highlighted sentences in a row, you need to add evidence and create a new paragraph.

For a greener editing process, you can use your computer's highlight function.

In this read-through:

1. Make sure you have signposts that alert your reader to why a paragraph or section exists and transitions connecting text to prior points, your thesis, and/or your supporting arguments.

2. Check whether each section and paragraph answers the question "so what?"
    i.   Is the relationship between each of your subarguments and the main thesis clear?
    ii. Do you know why you are reading a given paragraph, fact, or point?

3. Double-check that you have provided adequate support for every claim.
    i.   Are the sources credible? (see chapter 4 for more about credible sources).
    ii. Do the sources support the points for which you're citing them?
    iii. Have you written conclusory or editorial statements for which *no* objective support would be sufficient (e.g., "apples aren't as delicious as pears")?

4. You're almost done! If at all possible, go for a walk before your final read-through.

Paint It, Polish It, Put It on the Road: Third Read-Through

Now you're ready for the type of self-editing you've done before—reading closely and editing sentence by sentence. Here are some sentence-level tips for this stage.

1. Passive voice is a thing that should not be used by you. (Did that sentence annoy you? Good. That's why you *avoid passive voice*.)

    Writing refresher: When you write in passive voice, the subject of the sentence receives an action (the ball was hit by the batter). In active voice, the subject performs the action (the batter hit the ball).
2. Backward like Yoda write you should not.

3. Adverbs are the enemy. They add nothing to a point and sometimes reflect a gap in evidence.

   a. The worst offenders are "clearly" and "obviously." If it's clear or obvious, you shouldn't need to write it; if it isn't, you need to support it with evidence.

   b. "Essentially" is meaningless filler.

4. Write as if every prepositional phrase costs one dollar. "The truth of Seidman's point is illustrated by his focus on the shameful values of the founders" is a poorly written sentence. Instead, try this: "Seidman states that because the founders accepted slavery and excluded women from voting, we should not use the Constitution they wrote to solve modern problems."

5. Vary your sentence length. It can be difficult to write short sentences about complex material. Sometimes students write long sentences in an attempt to imitate sophisticated academic writing. Writing that includes sentences of varying lengths is easier to process and often more pleasurable to read. When doing your sentence-level read-through and edits, be on the lookout for unusually long sentences. You might find it useful to highlight your sentence and check the word count at the bottom of your screen. If your sentence is over 25 words or contains several phrases separated by commas, consider cutting it in two (or simplifying it).

6. Your reader should not get the impression that you wrote only one draft and did not check your work. Proofread and eliminate grammatical errors, misspellings, and prose or structure issues listed above.

Congratulations! Your paper is ready to go.

TAKING YOUR SECOND PAPER TO THE NEXT LEVEL

WHEN YOU'RE THERE

You can go to office hours as many times as you need to. Particularly in your first year, you might need to go before you turn in a paper and after you get it back.

Many first-year students feel anxious waiting for their first paper grade. That's normal. In fact, you might find yourself worrying about your first paper grade in each new course as you work to meet increasingly high expectations in your college career. That's okay, too. The important thing is to remain in charge of your writing development, using the feedback you receive to grow as a writer.

When your professor returns your paper, don't just look at the grade; read the feedback, too. Learning *why* you earned that grade will help you improve your next paper. Compare the professor's comments to the standards for college academic writing and the paper checklist on page 97. What was missing? If your professor tells you that you didn't support your claims with evidence, you know you need to focus on that more next time.

FAST FACT

Research shows that students who set an explicit goal for themselves perform better in school.[ii]

After you read your professor's feedback (or if they didn't give you that much feedback, which sometimes happens), go to office hours. Yes, *again*. This time, ask your professor to help you understand what you need to do to take your paper to the next level. Many universities also offer writing support through tutoring and writing centers (see chapter 8).

After I returned the first assignment in one of my first-year courses, a student came to my office hours with her paper, on which she'd earned a B+. She respectfully asked, "What do I need to do to get an A in this class?" I told her that to take her writing to the next level, she needed to focus more on the structure of her arguments and showed her a few places where she could have provided more context for the information she shared. Though she had come to talk about the paper, I also told her that although her contributions in class were thoughtful, I wanted to hear even more from her. I recommended that she take notes on the readings and speak up about the ways the readings related to my questions. She took notes on our conversation, thanked me, and went back and did everything I recommended. She earned an A and later worked with me on an important project. I'll always remember that conversation, and often share this story with my classes.

—COLLEGE PROFESSOR

Even if you earn an A on your paper, you should still be looking to improve. Your 200- and 300-level courses will require longer and more complex papers, and your professors are likely to apply tougher standards when they grade. Look at the feedback and challenge yourself to incorporate it into your next assignment.

DO BEFORE YOU GO

- Consider the types of assignments you've been asked to write. Do they include original research? Were you asked to make an original argument? How much experience do you have writing a persuasive paper?
- Consider the feedback you've received on papers over the years. What do your teachers say you need to improve? Do you sometimes get called out for stating opinions passionately but not proving your points? Have you been told you need to write more clearly?
- Set a goal for your writing and plan to use your school's resources to help you meet it.

***

We've found that students who use the strategies and habits of mind you learned in chapters 5, 6, and 7 are more likely to succeed (and less likely to become extremely stressed) in their courses. That being said, you don't have to tackle your college academics alone. Your college will offer resources including writing assistance, disability supports, technology, and more. In fact, the most successful college students learn when and how to use academic support services. Remember—adulting isn't about not needing help; it's about knowing when you need help and seeking it out when you do. In chapter 8, you'll learn about the types of academic support you might find on your campus.

8

KNOW YOUR NETWORK:
ACADEMIC SUPPORT

In all likelihood, you will struggle in at least one of your classes. Know that this is normal. Almost everyone will, although they probably won't let on. Admissions didn't make a mistake. You deserve to be at your college, and you will be successful. It might just be bumpy at first. Ask for help, and realize that struggling doesn't mean you're failing.

—COLLEGE ADMINISTRATOR

s you learned in detail in chapter 4, college coursework is different from high school work in significant ways, including:

- You will read more and write often.
- Professors will expect you to understand the material when you arrive in class.
- Because most classes meet between one and three times per week, you learn the material in larger chunks.

- You are expected to demonstrate higher-order thinking, not just comprehension.

Fortunately, your college has resources to support you as you transition to new challenges as a first-year student and throughout your college career. The resources and services in this chapter are usually included in your tuition.

In this chapter, you will:

1. Learn about the variety of academic support resources that colleges typically offer.

2. Familiarize yourself with your college's academic support resources, programs, and policies.

3. Start taking steps to arrange for resources you know you'll need.

COLLEGE LIBRARY SYSTEM

In the past, I've told students to come to the library when they have a question or feel stuck. Increasingly, I've started telling them to swing by even when they are pretty sure they have it all figured out. We all get comfortable with a favorite database, search engine, or search terms. Talking to a third party about your work can help you find the things you didn't realize you were looking for.

—COLLEGE LIBRARIAN

Your university library system is one of the most useful resources on campus. There you will find professionals with extensive experience both in research and teaching research, technology resources, online access to academic and research articles spanning every topic, and people who are ready to support you in mastering library use.

KNOW BEFORE YOU GO

- How do you access the university library system online portal for college students?
- What are the library's building hours (they are often open 24 hours) and librarian support hours?

- Is there an online system you can use to get help from the university librarians?

Asking for help is one of the scariest things that college brings with it, but you have to learn how to do it. This goes for all aspects of college. You will need to ask professors for help, so go to office hours early on so your professor knows you and knows that you are open to help and serious about the class.

—COLLEGE STUDENT

PROFESSORS AND TEACHING ASSISTANTS

As you learned in chapter 5, it's important to develop a professional, productive relationship with your college professors. As a start, you should be aware that your professors are the first line of support in your academic work. You don't need to have a problem in class to look to your professors and TAs as a resource. You can look to them for guidance on how to succeed in your classes from day one. Attending office hours is the first step.

TUTORING AND WRITING CENTERS

Go to the writing help center, your professors, or even the library if there is an assignment you need help with and that you want to do well on. These resources are here for your benefit, so use them.

—COLLEGE STUDENT

If school wasn't hard, we probably wouldn't learn as much from it. It's okay to need extra help with classes. In high school, you might have sought tutoring from your teacher or a community volunteer at school, or your parents might have found someone to work with you at home.

Although your professors and TAs are a great place to start when you need assistance in a course, they typically hold office hours only a few hours per week. For extensive one-on-one support, your university likely also offers access to subject matter tutors, language assistance (in English or the language you are studying), writing assistance, and supplemental instruction for common courses that are known to challenge students (such as macroeconomics or organic chemistry).

These services are typically free and available most days, either by appointment or on a walk-in basis.

KNOW BEFORE YOU GO

- Where are the tutoring and writing centers, what are their hours, and how do you make an appointment?
- Is there a separate tutoring center for courses in your major or discipline?
- Are there specialized tutoring services for students who are not native English speakers? For athletes? For first-generation students? For students with disabilities?
- Does your college offer additional help specifically for any of your first-semester courses, such as introductory calculus, economics, or chemistry?

DO BEFORE YOU GO

- Bookmark the tutoring and writing centers' websites on your browser.
- Add academic support contact information to your phone.

ACADEMIC ADVISING

Planning your course load in college can be tricky. Your curriculum may include core requirements, courses required for your major (and minor, if applicable), electives, and possibly labs, internships for credit, and study abroad. Academic advisers work with you to plan your education, set your schedule, and more.

At most schools, you will consult with the academic advising office about the following:

- Course registration
- Declaring or changing your major
- Fulfilling major requirements
- Fulfilling core curriculum requirements
- Arranging to have advanced placement or IB credits applied to your core or major requirements
- Planning to study abroad
- Dealing with academic probation, incomplete courses, or leaves of absence
- Utilizing and coordinating your other academic support resources

Increasingly, colleges and universities have specialized advising offices dedicated to first-year students. Many have academic advisers in each school division (i.e., the engineering, nursing, or business school) or in each academic department.

DO BEFORE YOU GO

Your school's first-year advising office might contact you over the summer. If so, read what they send and take advantage of their invitations to get in touch with them before orientation.

- Who are the academic advisers for first-year students and/or students in your intended major?
- What are their phone numbers and email addresses?

DISABILITY SUPPORT AND ACCESS

Americans born after 1990 are often called the ADA Generation, after the Americans with Disabilities Act, a civil rights law that opened new doors for students with all kinds of disabilities—from chronic illnesses and sensory disabilities to injuries and mental health disabilities.

As a student, you have a right to equal access to your education regardless of disability, and your college has dedicated support services to help make this happen.

Examples of disability supports and accommodations are:

- Closed captioning for videos and films assigned in classes
- A nondistracting environment in which to take exams
- Excused absences and extra support for disability-related leave
- Adaptive technology such as screen readers or amplification devices
- Supplemental tutoring
- Use of a laptop for note taking or exams

If you had disability accommodations in high school, you likely had a document called an Individualized Education Plan (IEP) or a 504 plan (named for Section 504 of the Rehabilitation Act) tailored to your particular needs.

At most US public schools, a team of school staff—typically including teachers and counselors—works with the student and family to develop these plans and report on progress. At college, your professors (and the school as a whole) are legally required to honor your disability accommodations but will not be on a team that develops them. Instead, you will work with your school's disability support staff to put accommodations in place, and then be responsible for informing your professor of what they are.

Here is a typical process for academic accommodations:

1. Contact the disability services center and fill out a request for accommodations.

2. Submit the required documentation of your disability, which should be a letter from your healthcare professional or counselor, and might also include your high school 504 plan or IEP.

3. Meet with a disability services staff member to discuss your requested accommodations. The staff will then prepare a plan for you, often in the form of a letter, describing the academic accommodations to which you are entitled.

NOTE: This process is confidential. The disability support office and staff may only provide information about you or your accommodations to people who are required to receive the information.

It is your responsibility to present your accommodations plan or letter to each professor in order to secure classroom and testing accommodations. Use this information as a reference when you are contacting your professors.

You Must:

- Provide documentation of your right to an accommodation.

- Contact them in a timely manner so they can ask follow-up questions and set up accommodations.

You Don't Have To:

- Disclose your disability. Your professor is legally required to comply with your accommodations plan but does not have a right to your personal history or medical information.

- Apologize or phrase your contact as a request. Equal access is your right.

Here is a sample email to your professor about accommodations:

Dear Professor Lopez,

I hope your semester is off to a good start. My name is Madison Williams, and I am in your Chemistry 101 course this semester.

I have accommodations for exams, including that I take tests in a quiet space. I've attached my letter from the Academic Accessibility Center, which describes my accommodations. I will contact you and the AAC before the midterm to arrange to take the test there. Please let me know if you have any questions or would like me to come in and discuss my accommodations during office hours.

Thank you for your help.

Sincerely,
Madison Williams

KNOW BEFORE YOU GO

- Who coordinates academic accommodations for students with disabilities?
- What is the process, including documentation requirements, for requesting accommodations?
- What is the process for informing professors about your accommodations?
- Does your school require you to make reservations for each exam you take in the disability center?

DO BEFORE YOU GO

- Gather your documentation, including letters from your medical or mental health professionals.
- Begin the process of registering for accommodations.
- If you have questions about the process, call the disability services office and ask for help.

SUPPORT FOR STUDENT ATHLETES

Balancing a competitive sport with your college course work (and your life) can be challenging. You will want to pay particular attention to the time management techniques in chapters 5 and 9. As described below, your university will also have resources to help you meet eligibility requirements and thrive in school.

NCAA Standards

The National Collegiate Athletic Association (NCAA) sets standards for student athletes to be eligible to play. Divisions within the NCAA set the standards for eligibility to play in that division. Student athletes must complete a set percentage of course work toward their degree each year, maintain enrollment in a minimum number of credits, and maintain a certain GPA. The NCAA's requirements for student athletes can be found online at http://www.ncaa.org/student-athletes. Check your division's website for eligibility requirements.

University Resources

Many universities have dedicated resources for supporting student athletes in their academic careers. Examples of student athlete support services include:

- Formal permission to be excused from class for travel and games
- Alternative exam proctoring arrangements for when athletic obligations conflict with exams
- Additional advising and academic coaching
- Life skills coaching, including support with time management
- Career development help

KNOW BEFORE YOU GO

- If there is not a separate office for student athletes, where do you look for these resources? (The academic advising office or campus life offices might include student athlete support.)

- What is your school's policy about classroom absences and exam conflicts for student athletes?
- How does your athletic schedule affect your first-semester classes?

DO BEFORE YOU GO

- If the school has not already started the process, contact your student athlete support representative and introduce yourself.
- Begin the process of securing a letter from your team or student athletics office that you can share with your professors.
- When you introduce yourself to your professors by email (see page 78), include information about your athletic obligations, if it is relevant.

Contacting Your Professors About Your Athletic Obligations

Do:

- Assure your professors that you will stay current with the course readings and seek class notes from a classmate.
- Indicate the dates when you will have an excused absence for a sport.
- Provide documentation, such as a letter from your team, as your school instructs you to.
- Go to office hours frequently.

Do *not*:

- State that because of your commitments, you might not always be ready for class or could be tired in class.
- Ask to be excused from required assignments such as group projects, even if practices and travel make it difficult to work with a group.
- Expect the professor to give you an individualized catch-up lesson after every absence.

TECHNOLOGY SUPPORT

When you head to college, you're not only moving to a new town and studying in a new building; you're changing your online "homes," too. Here are examples of college-specific technology you'll use:

- University email account, which you should receive shortly after you enroll.
- Web academic portals such as Blackboard, MYEDU, ecollege, Canvas, and others, where your professors will post syllabi, course readings, and assignments
- WiFi networks
- Online portals for payroll (if you work for your school), financial aid, course registration, meal plan balances, and tuition payments
- Accounts for printing
- Library research accounts

Make sure you are familiar with these tools and where to get help with them.

WHEN YOU'RE THERE

Your professors will generally sympathize if you run into a technology problem, but don't not ask them to serve as tech support. Inform your professor when a tech problem has caused an unavoidable delay, and let them know you have already reached out to technology support to solve the problem.

INTERNATIONAL STUDENT SUPPORT

FAST FACT

Did you know you're not alone? There are almost one million international students studying at US colleges and universities.[iii]

If you are traveling to the US from another country to study, you are more likely than ever to find services and supports tailored to your needs. Your academic needs could include:

- Support with language, if English is not your first language.
- Information about aspects of US government and history that are covered in American schools and professors assume students know.
- Information about how to get college credit for courses taken in your home country.

SEEKING HELP

Knowing where to go for help makes a big difference to your success. In fact, knowing your college has all these resources for you should boost your confidence as you start your college career. Knowing *when* to seek support for your academics is important, too. Our advice is to make use of the resources your school has even when you don't feel you're struggling, and regularly consider whether you could be doing better and should seek additional support.

Academic Support: Know Where to Go

ISSUE	RESOURCE
You don't understand course readings.	Professor or TA (office hours or professional email)
The course web portal is not accepting your submission.	IT support
There are no spots available in a required course for your major.	Academic advisers
You need to take exams in a quiet room, on a computer.	Disability support and access office
Your first draft of a paper is unclear.	Writing center

Consider these questions on a regular basis:

- **READING:** Do you find it difficult to complete the readings before every class? Do you understand them?
- **CLASS PARTICIPATION:** Does it feel like class discussion is over your head? Do you feel anxious that if you're called on, you won't know the answer?
- **BALANCING OBLIGATIONS:** Are you finding it difficult to balance your athletic, work, military service, or other obligations with your classwork?

If the answer to any of these questions is yes, then you should seek out academic support resources.

You will probably find that you need different resources depending on your course load. You're more likely to need extensive support from the library when you have research papers. If you use the writing center early in your college career, you might find that you need it less later. Some students will need more tutoring support in math than the humanities, while some are the opposite. Start each semester with the assumption that you *will* make use of the resources your school has available. You won't regret talking to a professor, tutor, or librarian, even if they tell you you're right on track (which actually feels pretty good).

We hope that this part of the book has made college work less mysterious and given you more confidence that you'll be able to understand and meet the demands of your academic career. By using effective academic techniques and your school's resources, you can and will succeed.

However, the most important resource you have is *you*. To be the best professional and student you can be, you need to look after yourself. Your health and wellness—physical, mental, and spiritual—are critical to your success and happiness. In college and in life, you will be the one responsible for this. In part III, you'll learn about keeping yourself healthy and safe and accessing care.

PART III

TAKE CARE OF YOU

In this section of the book, we'll spend time discussing your wellness, health, and safety as you become a college student and take control of your own physical and mental healthcare. We'll introduce you to the resources and individuals on your campus that will support you in this journey. You'll learn about the challenges of healthy eating, sleeping, time management, and maintaining (or finding) your spirituality as you immerse yourself in the busy life of a college student.

We'll share tips for maintaining productive and holistic wellness habits in college. Then we'll turn to your specific physical and mental health needs, explain how you can access healthcare resources on and off campus, and thoroughly understand your health insurance (giving you an edge on 95 percent of people in the country!). We'll conclude with an important discussion on campus safety and present information on what items to purchase, what behaviors to practice, and how to prepare to be the sole person responsible for your own safety and well-being in college.

9

EAT, SLEEP,
PRAY, PLAY: WELLNESS

The transition to college and adulting can feel complicated, and it can be harder to focus on the simpler things—sleeping, eating, and taking time for what brings you joy and meaning. Many incoming students are just as worried about the "freshman 15" as they are about planning their first fifteen-page paper. In this chapter, you'll learn how to incorporate wellness essentials into your college life.

USING YOUR CAMPUS WELLNESS CENTER

Your campus will most likely offer a center or department that focuses on wellness and aims to promote the holistic well-being of students through comprehensive and collaborative programming, peer education, and the sharing of accurate and relevant health information and resources. This center might be a part of the campus health center, a health promotion department, or a counseling center. It might also be its own separate entity, staffed by professionals and peer educators alike.

Most campus centers that focus on student wellness provide education around some if not all of the following: alcohol and other drugs (AOD), sexual health, sexual violence prevention programs, physical fitness, nutrition, and mindfulness. Confidential consultation is usually available, and the centers often provide condoms and other sexual health resources for students free of charge. Campus wellness resources most frequently focus on developing positive healthy habits, supporting student lifestyles, teaching about self-care, and reducing risk behaviors.

You might find that your campus does not provide access to some of these resources, especially those related LGBTQ wellness, reproductive health, or sexual health programming and support. National organizations and programs such as the Human Rights Campaign's Healthcare Equality Index (https://www.hrc.org/hei), Health Professionals Advancing LGBT Equality (http://www.glma.org), and the National Association of Obstetricians and Gynecologists (https://www.acog.org) are available to connect you with local resources.

PREPARING FOR THE CHALLENGES OF HEALTHY EATING IN COLLEGE

While living at home, it is likely that someone else has planned, shopped, and maybe even prepared your meals for you. You probably had a lunch period at school at a set time. Perhaps you were expected to set the table or join in a family meal at a certain time. Someone might have even made sure that you were eating your fruits and vegetables. College eating is a *big* change, and planning for this in advance will make your transition easier.

Eating well and healthy in college is not always an easy feat, and many first-year students are surprised at how different their eating becomes after leaving home. Fresh fruit and vegetables are not always readily available on your campus meal plan, and the cultural/regional foods that you grew up with might not be easily accessible. Perhaps for the first time you're making all your own decisions about what you should and shouldn't eat. You're surrounded by snacks and sweets, you're often in a rush, and controlling what you consume without full access to a kitchen can be a challenge.

DO BEFORE YOU GO

Before heading to college, research if your residence hall has a kitchen you can use and if they provide cooking essentials. If so, gather some recipes for easy meals you enjoy at home. If not, look for some microwaveable and no-cook meal recipes to bring with you so that you can prepare food in your room at school.

Mindful Eating Starts Before You Get to College

You will eventually learn to plan your meals around your class schedule, but it is also important to make a concerted effort to remember to actually eat *meals*, not just snacks. All colleges will have some gym or fitness center that students can access, so you can keep in shape. However, this is balanced by the many opportunities to indulge in unhealthy food behaviors, and—let's face it—eating fast food is often easy and accessible on campus.

WHEN YOU'RE THERE

Regularly take a piece of fruit to go when leaving the campus cafeteria—it's included in your meal plan and most colleges allow students to do so when they are exiting.

Before you leave for college, pay special attention to which foods and drinks work for your body and which don't, since you will now be making food decisions completely by yourself. Ask yourself how what you eat affects your mood, your sleep, and your energy. Maybe too many carbs hurt your stomach. Maybe dairy makes you congested. Take notes on what you find, so when you are in college you can make informed decisions about the food you purchase and eat. You might choose to use one of many free online food journals or apps to make this task easier.

Over the summer, you should also take a look at your exercise routine and, if you have not already done so, see if you can get into a workout pattern before you leave for college. First-year students who already have a healthy exercise regimen in place seem to find it relatively easy to follow the same schedule in college. However, students who establish an exercise plan for the first time in college find that it is just one more "new thing" to take on.

KNOW BEFORE YOU GO

- Most US colleges and universities offer varsity sports, intramural sports, and club sports.

- If you will not already be competing as a varsity athlete in college, take a look at the list of club and intramural sports that your school offers and see if one interests you.

- Check out the options for athletic activities you may have enjoyed as a child, sports you were involved in during high school, or even something you have never tried before.

See chapter 18 for detailed information about sports and fitness opportunities on campus.

College is *also* the place where you can start establishing your own eating patterns, ones that are healthy and leave you feeling energized. The summer before college is a great time to educate yourself about nutrition and begin to make some choices before your first year begins.

You Shouldn't:

- Bring a bunch of high-preservative, high-calorie junk foods and candy to college; if it is in your room, you're more likely to eat it without thinking.

- Plan all your weekly shopping at a local gourmet market or even at the on-campus market, as you will be overcharged.

- Buy more fast-spoiling foods (like berries or bananas) than you will eat.

You Should:

- Stock up on staples for your college room that include healthy foods with a long shelf life, such as nut butter, dried fruit, popcorn, and granola.

- Locate a large local grocery store near campus to stock your minifridge when you arrive.

- Plan to buy fruit that stays fresh for weeks, such as apples and oranges.

Late-Night Snacking in College

You've probably heard that late-night snacking isn't good for you, but do remember that the hours you keep in college will be quite different from those you've had in high school. Late-night eating often becomes part a social activity or a group study session. You can still make healthy choices, such as popcorn or dark chocolate rather than greasy cheese pizza. Finally, it's extremely important to eat three regular meals. If you do, you'll be less likely to crave snacks late in the evening.

GETTING ENOUGH SLEEP

Few high school students keep very healthy sleep schedules. The summer before you head off to college is the time to get your sleeping on track. In college, you'll be busy with your classes, social life, co-curricular activities, and perhaps work commitments, but you will not have the seven or so academic classes you had in high school.

While late nights may be unavoidable during finals, it is important
to remember that a solid night of sleep will help you stay healthy. As you
did in high school, in college it's important to balance your sleep
schedule, your assignments, and the rest of your life.

One big difference, however, is that when you're at home,
chances are, the house is quiet when you're ready to settle in for the
night. There might even be someone encouraging you to go to bed.
In college, your residence hall could be noisy when you're trying to get
to sleep, and you might be tempted to hang out with friends who are
up at all hours. It's easy to sacrifice sleep to spend more time with
peers when you should be heading to bed.

It's possible you and your roommate will keep different hours. If
this is the case and you're having trouble keeping your sleep schedule, you should communicate with your roommate. See chapter 2
for help with maintaining a positive relationship with your roommate (while taking care of yourself).

Develop a sleep routine so that you don't wear yourself out. It's
important to get in a consistent amount of sleep to function
properly throughout the week of work ahead. You don't want to
oversleep, miss your class, or miss something important, so a
consistent sleep schedule will allow you to wake up easier. It's also
not just a matter of waking up with ease, but also waking up feeling
refreshed.

—COLLEGE STUDENT

Technology and Sleep

The blue light emitted from electronics tricks your brain into thinking it's daytime, which makes it more difficult to fall asleep. Sleep ex-

perts recommend shutting down your technology at least 30 minutes before going to bed. That's tough for most teens and young adults to do. Summer is the time to get in the habit and practice for first-year sleep success. Shutting down is the best choice, but if you have to work late, check to see if your device has a feature that reduces blue light.

Practice Napping the Proper Way

Napping was a big part of your life when you were little, and it's cool again in college. If you are not someone who naps regularly, practice at home before you leave for college. Yes, there actually *is* a proper way to take a nap so that you reap the benefits of the recharge. It's suggested that if you do take a short nap, you limit it to 20 to 30 minutes and do so before four p.m. to avoid the groggy feeling that occurs when you're awakened during a sleep cycle. If you have the time for a longer nap, try not to lengthen it beyond 90 minutes, which is the length of an average person's sleep cycle.

MANAGING YOUR TIME TO UNDERSTAND YOUR PRIORITIES AND REDUCE STRESS

Asking for help is one of the scariest things that college brings with it, but you have to learn how to do it. Asking for help can oftentimes seem like admitting to defeat, but it is the exact opposite; it shows that you are willing to do what it takes to succeed. The resources on campus help strengthen people's confidence in college and their newfound "freedom" and responsibility.

—COLLEGE STUDENT

Of course, it's hard to imagine how you will manage your time on campus until you have a better idea what your class schedule will be. However, the summer before your leave for college is a great time to take on the 168 Assignment. This exercise is commonly used by academic support centers and first-year experience courses on college campuses across the United States. Many first-year students find it quite helpful. We strongly suggest that you try this exercise *before* you head off to school so you have a leg up on time management before your first semester begins.

The 168 Assignment

Fill out the chart (p. 130), considering a "typical" week for you this summer, recording your activities for every one of the 168 hours in that given week. Assign a category to each block of time, choosing them from the list below or creating new ones that reflect your own life and schedule. Suggested categories include:

- Grooming (washing/getting ready)
- Eating
- Sleeping/napping
- Social media
- Cleaning living environment
- Relaxing alone
- Socializing with others (outside of meals)
- Practicing skill(s)
- Attending a class
- Studying
- Exercising
- Religious/spiritual practice or observation

- Co-curricular activities (academic, social, cultural)
- Service/volunteer work
- Paid work

Next, calculate the total number of hours you spent on activities within each category. Make sure the sum of your hours across all categories is 168. Feel free to delete, combine, or add categories to personalize the experience. This assignment is intended to serve as a tool for your self-assessment, not for another's judgment, so be honest with yourself.

After your chart is complete, consider the following questions:

- How did you spend the majority of your time each week?
- Did any of your category totals surprise you?
- Can you identify your personal time-wasters? (Note that not all relaxing hours are considered "time-wasters"; some are beneficial for personal health and wellness.)
- Should you/are you able to reprioritize any of the categories so that they might be beneficial to you during your first semester of college?

WHEN YOU'RE THERE

Once you know the times and days your classes will meet during your first semester of college, plug in your class schedule to get a better idea of what your college 168 will look like.

How Do I Spend My 168?

MON					
6:00 AM		2:00 PM		10:00 PM	
7:00 AM		3:00 PM		11:00 PM	
8:00 AM		4:00 PM		12:00 AM	
9:00 AM		5:00 PM		1:00 AM	
10:00 AM		6:00 PM		2:00 AM	
11:00 AM		7:00 PM		3:00 AM	
12:00 PM		8:00 PM		4:00 AM	
1:00 PM		9:00 PM		5:00 AM	

TUES					
6:00 AM		2:00 PM		10:00 PM	
7:00 AM		3:00 PM		11:00 PM	
8:00 AM		4:00 PM		12:00 AM	
9:00 AM		5:00 PM		1:00 AM	
10:00 AM		6:00 PM		2:00 AM	
11:00 AM		7:00 PM		3:00 AM	
12:00 PM		8:00 PM		4:00 AM	
1:00 PM		9:00 PM		5:00 AM	

WED					
6:00 AM		2:00 PM		10:00 PM	
7:00 AM		3:00 PM		11:00 PM	
8:00 AM		4:00 PM		12:00 AM	
9:00 AM		5:00 PM		1:00 AM	
10:00 AM		6:00 PM		2:00 AM	
11:00 AM		7:00 PM		3:00 AM	
12:00 PM		8:00 PM		4:00 AM	
1:00 PM		9:00 PM		5:00 AM	

THUR					
6:00 AM		2:00 PM		10:00 PM	
7:00 AM		3:00 PM		11:00 PM	
8:00 AM		4:00 PM		12:00 AM	
9:00 AM		5:00 PM		1:00 AM	
10:00 AM		6:00 PM		2:00 AM	
11:00 AM		7:00 PM		3:00 AM	
12:00 PM		8:00 PM		4:00 AM	
1:00 PM		9:00 PM		5:00 AM	

FRI					
6:00 AM		2:00 PM		10:00 PM	
7:00 AM		3:00 PM		11:00 PM	
8:00 AM		4:00 PM		12:00 AM	
9:00 AM		5:00 PM		1:00 AM	
10:00 AM		6:00 PM		2:00 AM	
11:00 AM		7:00 PM		3:00 AM	
12:00 PM		8:00 PM		4:00 AM	
1:00 PM		9:00 PM		5:00 AM	

SAT					
6:00 AM		2:00 PM		10:00 PM	
7:00 AM		3:00 PM		11:00 PM	
8:00 AM		4:00 PM		12:00 AM	
9:00 AM		5:00 PM		1:00 AM	
10:00 AM		6:00 PM		2:00 AM	
11:00 AM		7:00 PM		3:00 AM	
12:00 PM		8:00 PM		4:00 AM	
1:00 PM		9:00 PM		5:00 AM	

SUN					
6:00 AM		2:00 PM		10:00 PM	
7:00 AM		3:00 PM		11:00 PM	
8:00 AM		4:00 PM		12:00 AM	
9:00 AM		5:00 PM		1:00 AM	
10:00 AM		6:00 PM		2:00 AM	
11:00 AM		7:00 PM		3:00 AM	
12:00 PM		8:00 PM		4:00 AM	
1:00 PM		9:00 PM		5:00 AM	

MEETING YOUR SPIRITUAL NEEDS IN COLLEGE

Spirituality helps you to figure out what matters in life. When you're spending so much of your time studying, working, applying for internships, and getting involved on campus, it's easy to get burned out. Knowing what matters to you and why is an important part of leading a balanced life and ultimately being a better student.

—UNIVERSITY CHAPLAIN

Spirituality is an overlooked part of wellness, and there is data to support that students who enter college with a set routine that meets their spiritual needs thrive in their new environment. There was even a multiyear research project out of UCLA's Higher Education Research Institute (HERI) that examined the importance of the spiritual development of undergraduate students during their college years.[iv] Many colleges are turning to include students' spiritual development as a core component of a liberal arts education.

There's more to wellness than feeding and resting your body (because there's more to you than just your body). Taking care of yourself means taking care of *all* of you. It's important to see the big picture—whether you call that spirituality, religion, mindfulness, or just being human. Here are some bigger-picture questions we encourage you to consider as you prepare for college (and when you're there):

- "What am I supposed to get out of college?"
- "How will I know if the choices I'm making in college are the right ones?"
- "What kind of adult do I want to be?"

Questioning What You've Known

One of the purposes of spiritual and religious practices is to offer comfort in times of stress and transition. For students who grew up in an organized religion with the rituals that accompanied it, college might be a time to solidify those practices or tweak them in a way that works for your new environment. You might be asking what organized religion means to you as a college student. Some first-year students report feeling stressed or burdened by expectations about their commitment to the religious practices that have been a steady part of their lives. Don't forget that college is also a time to explore new religious and spiritual practices, perhaps even for the first time.

On-Campus Spiritual Resources

All college campuses will offer some opportunities and physical space for spiritual learning, community, and observance for a host of religious and spiritual groups. Many college students find that joining a spiritual community on campus—or even simply using the campus chapel as a place to reflect—is an important part of their college life. Even if you don't consider yourself religious, you might find that your campus spiritual center has something for you; many host events and programs related to social justice, community service, and interfaith dialogue.

College chaplains have unique experience and training to serve the spiritual and personal wellness needs of college students and young adults. They combine both expertise with spiritual development and the student experience. In other words, they not only can help you while you're *in* college, they know how to help you *with* college.

KNOW BEFORE YOU GO

- Explore the religious and spiritual organizations that are offered on your campus by reading about these opportunities online.
- Check out the services, discussion groups, lectures, meditations, and student clubs of a religious group familiar to you or one you would like to explore when your first semester begins.
- What is your school's policy on addressing students' requests for religious accommodations?*
  - **ACADEMIC** (for example, missing class or receiving extra time to complete an assignment or test due to religious observance)

- **DIETARY** (for example, kosher or halal)
- **HOUSING** (for example, single-sex residence hall options)

*Note that both procedures and availability of accommodations will vary from school to school. Many will require a written request in advance.

Finding a Religious/Spiritual Community
Off Campus

Some students choose to join a religious or spiritual community off campus in the neighboring community that might better meet their needs. If this option is for you, don't forget to check out the public transportation or rideshare services available to reach the house of worship at the time the services are offered. Note that many congregations near college campuses provide rides free of charge for students so that they can attend services. We would suggest that you wait until you get to school to make the decision to join a house of worship off campus, but as always, being prepared in advance will help ease your transition.

DISCUSS BEFORE YOU GO

- **IS IT IMPORTANT TO YOU TO FIND A FAITH COMMUNITY THAT INCLUDES PEOPLE OF ALL AGES?** Most religious services on college campuses are geared toward the 18-to-22-year-old age bracket. For some students, a congregation that's multi-generational can provide a valuable perspective outside what is offered on campus. Do you want access to communicating/volunteering with senior citizens? Are you looking to work with children, such as teaching religious school?

- **DO YOU WANT YOUR NEW FAITH COMMUNITY TO BE SEPARATE FROM YOUR SCHOOL LIFE?** Some students report that they want their congregations to serve as a refuge from peer relationships. They feel that participating in a spiritual community separate from where they live and learn is a refreshing change. Others like meeting fellow students with similar religious backgrounds. Many enjoy the ease of participating in a religious/spiritual life that is right where they live on campus and find they are more willing to attend services and discussion groups regularly because it is so convenient.

- **WHAT WILL YOU DO IF NEITHER YOUR CAMPUS NOR YOUR NEW COLLEGE TOWN HAS A PLACE OF WORSHIP THAT MEETS YOUR NEEDS?** How will you stay connected to your spiritual community back home? Do you want to attend religious services or gatherings in a language other than English? Are you interested in a weekly service time, such as a Catholic Mass or Muslim call to worship that is not provided on your campus? If your campus has one nondenominational religious/spiritual sanctuary, will this work for your needs, or are you looking for a denomination-specific house of worship? Would you consider starting a religious/spiritually focused group on your campus if one does not exist?

Three easy ways to find a religious/spiritual community off campus:

- Contact your current house of worship and ask them to connect you with a congregation in your new city. Many religious leaders have colleagues and "sister congregations" throughout the United States.

- Search the internet; the houses of worship within that denomination will be listed. Email the religious/spiritual leader (see chapter 5 to learn to write a professional email). Introduce yourself and ask about attending services in their congregation when you get to town.

- Contact the religious leader or staff adviser of the denominational group with which you identify on your new campus and ask them for a referral to a local house of worship.

DISCUSS BEFORE YOU GO

Every family is different; discussing expectations in advance will help de-stress your transition away from those familiar practices. Before heading to college, we suggest discussing with your family what their expectations are:

- For your religious practices while you are away from home
- For your travel back home for observances and holidays
- About you finding a house of worship on or off campus

FINDING AN OFF-CAMPUS SUPPORT GROUP

Support groups are offered as a space where individuals with similar concerns can come together to share their stories, experiences, and lives in a way that helps reduce the feeling of suffering alone. Some organizations offer online support groups, discussion boards, blogs, and online communities as additional ways to connect with others in similar situations. These can be helpful additions to in-person support groups and can be especially helpful if there are no groups in your area.

Your university health, wellness, or counseling center may offer support groups focused on a variety of topics such as depression, sexual assault, anxiety, bereavement and grief, and LGBTQ support. However, campus support group options are often limited due to the complex schedules of college students, space requirement, or expertise of the college counselors. Your campus counseling center will be a great resource to help you find an off-campus support group to attend in the community, and your local Mental Health America affiliate (http://www.mentalhealthamerica.net/find-affiliate) is an excellent resource to assist you in finding support groups in your area.

Maintaining your wellness is a lifelong project. Once you're in college, you should remember to revisit your wellness habits from time to time as your schedule and responsibilities continue to change. Consider redoing your 168 exercise (see page 128), keeping track of your food and sleep, and meeting your spiritual and recreation needs. Health apps, journals, and on-campus health education programs can be extremely useful along the way. Part of adulting is knowing when and how to use expert resources; your campus health and wellness providers are there to help. In the next chapter, you'll learn how to meet your physical and mental health needs in college, access healthcare resources, and understand your insurance plan.

10

HEALTH 101:
ACCESS TO CARE IN SCHOOL

Although you are tasked with more responsibilities in college, your health remains a top priority. Without your health, you can't do anything, and your grades and social life are basically on hold. By taking care of yourself, you are allowing yourself to accomplish the most you can.

—COLLEGE STUDENT

PREPARING TO MANAGE YOUR HEALTH
AWAY FROM HOME

Before leaving for college, it is strongly recommended that you take a full healthcare inventory; see your medical/dental provider(s) and set up a plan for treatment and prescriptions so that you are prepared for your own self-care when you are away from home. Think about the person who has been arranging these things for you while you have been living at home. If this person is not you, the summer before you leave for college is the time to take on many of these responsibilities for yourself. What if you need a throat culture or chip a tooth while you are in college? Where should you go for treatment? Are you prepared for your first illness away from home? And how *does* your health insurance work?

This chapter will cover two major areas that you'll want to understand in order to manage your healthcare needs in college:

First, we'll focus on your own self-care, which includes seeing your health provider(s) before you leave for school for your pre-college visit; purchasing and packing healthcare-related items for your college room; learning what to do if you get sick away from home; and mental health counseling in college.

Second, you'll learn about how to get access to care through your campus health center and off-campus services. We'll cover detailed information about health insurance, including the different types of plans, seeing providers on and off campus, and the health insurance choices available to you by comparing your family's current plan and your college's health plan options.

THE PRE-COLLEGE VISIT

In order to assume responsibility for managing your health, it is imperative that you arrange for a pre-college visit with your medical provider. Ideally, this appointment will take place a few months before you leave for campus. Remember that this is an incredibly busy time for medical practices, so schedule your appointment as early as possible (right after high school graduation, if you can). The first step of adulting with your healthcare needs is to make your appointment(s) *by yourself.*

Your college or university will send you a list of the immunizations required for you to begin your first year, which you will need to bring to your appointment. It is important to understand that the immunizations your college requires might be different than what your home state required for you to attend high school.

Ideally in May, June, or July (if you are starting fall semester), schedule and attend your pre-college medical appointment(s). You should:

- Call the office(s) to arrange the appointment(s).
- Bring your medical insurance information with you.
- Bring the required copay.
- Bring your immunization form and any other health forms that your school requires. Don't forget to submit them.
- Inform your provider(s) that you are moving to college and provide your cell phone number, your new college email, and your mailing address.

What to Discuss at Your Appointment

If you are already eighteen, this appointment and follow-up discussion should be an open and confidential one between you and your medical provider. If you are under eighteen, although your parent or guardian has a legal right to be at this appointment, we would encourage you to use this opportunity to advocate for yourself and encourage an open and confidential conversation between you and your medical provider. If you have not done so before, this dialogue is great practice for having adult conversations in college without a family member present. Although your medical provider will guide the appointment with a list of questions and discussion points, it is your responsibility as an incoming college student to make sure that the following points are covered in your conversation:

- Your personal health history, including illnesses, surgeries, disabilities, and injuries
- A discussion of your family health history, including use of alcohol and drugs in your family, if known
- A review of your allergies
- A full understanding of any medications you are currently taking or treatments you are undergoing, including their purpose, dosage,

regularity, and any other medications that you should not take while you are on them

- How you will find a medical or mental health provider on campus or in your new city if needed

- Any symptoms that you should look for due to a condition you have or a medication you take (for example, if you have diabetes, you should contact a health provider if you see nail fungus)

- Your prescription renewals and challenges (for example, certain medications, including some for ADHD, cannot be prescribed across state lines)

- An honest discussion about your sexual health history and your sexual health needs in college

DO BEFORE YOU GO

If you know that you will need to see a medical or mental health professional at school or in your new city for a chronic condition (such as allergy shots or mental health counseling), *don't* wait until you arrive on campus to figure it out.

Work with your current practitioner (and, if applicable, your campus health center) to arrange a way to manage your needs when you are away from home.

In addition to your general practitioner, you should make sure that you schedule or have had recent appointments with any other healthcare providers, including your mental healthcare provider, allergist, dentist, orthodontist, therapist/counselor, ophthalmologist/optometrist, and gynecologist.

PACKING YOUR HEALTHCARE KIT

You *don't* want to have to go to the store to buy certain items when you actually feel sick, so in addition to your prescription medications (and refill information), stock up in advance on over-the-counter medications if you feel that you might use them in college. First, make sure:

1. You aren't allergic to any of them
2. None of them interact with the medications you are already taking
3. They haven't expired (if you're stocking up from your home medicine cabinet)

Always take over-the-counter medications with caution after carefully reading the dosage instructions. Make sure you don't double up on active ingredients if you take multiple medications at once, especially if you are taking a multisymptom medication (such as one that treats a fever, congestion, and coughing). We strongly suggest that you write down the time you took a medication and the dosage; you are more likely to forget if your mind is foggy when you are sick.

Consider purchasing items for safer sex, including what might be relevant to you, such as condoms, lubricant, dental dams, and/or a one-step emergency contraceptive. You can also find out if any of these items are available for free to students on your campus (they often are).

College Health and Emergency Kit

Acetaminophen

Adhesive bandages

Allergy medicine

Antacid tablets

Antibiotic ointment

Antihistamine

Antinausea medication

Bottle brush to clean out your water bottle (glass bottle suggested)

Cold sore medication

Contact lens care items

Cortisone cream

Cough drops

Cough medicine

Decongestant

Digital thermometer

Dish soap for washing your eating/drinking items

Disinfectant cleaner

Extra pair of eyeglasses

Extra toothbrush

Eyeglass repair kit

Hand sanitizer

Ibuprofen

Orthodontic appliances or supplies

Saline nasal spray

Comforts-of-Home Kit

Heating pad (electric or microwaveable)

Honey

Ice pack to be kept in the freezer of your minifridge

Instant or canned soup

Tea

Warm blanket

DO BEFORE YOU GO

Arrange for Your Prescriptions to Be Refilled and/or Transferred

- Check whether your campus health center will accept prescriptions from your doctor(s).
- If not, research pharmacies and/or doctors near campus that will accept your new prescriptions or set up a mailing plan.
- Find out whether your plan includes a mail-order pharmacy.

Reduce Your Chances of Getting Sick in College

Living in such close proximity to others in a residence hall exposes you to a plethora of germs.

Here are some easy ways to regularly reduce your chances of getting sick in college:

- **WASH YOUR HANDS** regularly with warm water and soap; use hand sanitizer when hand-washing is not an option.

- **USE DISINFECTANT** when you clean your room.

- **DON'T SHARE** drinks, food, makeup, or towels with others.

- **KEEP YOUR DISTANCE** when your roommates and friends get sick, and stay away from any objects they touch.

- **REPLACE YOUR TOOTHBRUSH** every semester and replace it or wash it thoroughly if you have been sick.

- **WASH YOUR WATER BOTTLE DAILY** with very hot water and soap if a dishwasher is not available.

FAST FACT

You might be able to find low-cost or free dental care through dental schools or dental hygiene schools, or at a community clinic. For information about free or low-cost dental care, visit www.hhs.gov.

WHEN YOU'RE THERE

Avoid the flu: Most colleges will advertise annual flu vaccines in the early fall. Make sure to get one on your campus or at an urgent care clinic or pharmacy near your school where they are free or inexpensive.

DEALING WITH PHYSICAL ILLNESS AWAY FROM HOME

Getting sick when you were at home and juggling high school was bad enough, but getting sick in college without a medicine cabinet, an accessible kitchen, a familiar medical provider, and family members to care for you is even more challenging. Being prepared for your first illness away from home (because at some point, you will get sick) will make it that much easier.

When you do get sick at school, communicate: reach out and let your roommate, friends, or RA know you are not feeling well. They can bring you meals and drinks, pick up medications for you, and check in on you to see how you are feeling. Do your best to drink fluids such as water, juice, and electrolytes to counteract dehydration from a fever, and avoid alcohol and caffeinated beverages. Sleep as much as you can—one of the most effective ways to aid recovery is to let your body rest. Your roommate(s) might feel that leaving you in the room alone is a good idea for everyone involved. They can stay in a friend's room so that you can get some sleep and they can stay away from your germs. You might have to do the same thing for your roommate during the year.

Your Campus Health Center

Most schools have a campus health center. At some schools, it is a small facility that can handle simple injuries, common illnesses like strep throat, and basic preventive care such as contraception. At others, the health center could be a full-service clinic. Other schools do not have a health clinic on campus, but instead send students to a clinic in the community. Some universities with medical schools have health centers connected with the university hospital. Familiarize yourself with your health center's services, hours of operation, location, and contact information.

DO BEFORE YOU GO

If you will have regular preventative healthcare needs at school, acquaint yourself with any of these that are applicable to you:

- Know the campus address and mailroom hours if you will have prescription medications or supplies sent directly to you.
- Find out if your campus health center can refill your prescriptions for you or if there is a pharmacy near your school where you can pick them up (and that you know how to get there).

KNOW BEFORE YOU GO

If you see a medical provider on campus or in your college town, the experience might be different than what is familiar at home. For example, you might be treated by a nurse practitioner or a physician assistant rather than a doctor. These are all trained medical professionals.

When It's More Than a Cold

Many illnesses, such as common colds, have no "cure" and, with the help of some symptom relievers, sleep, and plenty of fluids, they will simply need to run their course. But there are other illnesses, such as strep throat, bronchitis, mononucleosis, and flu, that require medical attention. According to the American Academy of Pediatrics, the following symptoms could be serious:

- A fever of 102°F or higher
- Pain in the abdomen that will not go away
- A persistent cough, chest pain, or trouble breathing
- A very sore throat
- Pain in your ears or sinuses
- A persistent fever
- Stiff neck
- Severe headache
- A flat, pink, red, or purple rash
- Nausea and vomiting
- Sensitivity to light
- Headache
- Swollen lymph nodes (glands) in the neck
- Extreme tiredness
- Pain or any other symptoms that worry you or last longer than you think they should

If you experience any of these symptoms, make sure to go to the student health center, a physician, clinic, or the emergency room as soon as possible. It's important to tell the medical provider about all your symptoms and concerns, not just the ones they have asked about. Make sure to express yourself clearly so that they understand the severity of your symptoms.

Handling Your Academics When You Are Sick in College

When you were sick in high school before you turned eighteen, your family probably needed to write a note to excuse you from your classes, explain your tardiness, or allow you to be dismissed early for a medical appointment. In college, there's no note to be had—it's up to you to make the decision if you are too sick to attend class or complete an assignment on time. Of course, as a college student, you should do everything you can to avoid missing class, but sometimes, your body tells you to slow down, and you must listen to it. You also want to respect the health of your classmates and professor.

Make sure you communicate with your professors and TAs if you are sick. You should also familiarize yourself with the rules each professor sets for required notification when missing a class due to an illness or a medical appointment, so check your syllabi, and ask the professor before the semester starts if the information isn't on the syllabus. Make sure to keep up with your readings, get notes from a friend in class, and focus on getting yourself better.

SEEKING MENTAL HEALTH COUNSELING IN COLLEGE

College is an exciting and rewarding time, but it is also a major life transition, and many college students experience stress, depression, and/or anxiety. If you had counseling before college or begin counseling in college, you aren't alone . . . and you are doing a great thing for yourself.

PRO-TIP

If you have had the ongoing support of a counselor, psychologist, or psychiatrist in the past, you will likely benefit from continued treatment, as least during the first semester as you transition to college life. We strongly suggest that you do not give up a resource that has worked well for you.

Learn about your college or university's resources for mental healthcare and counseling:

- **DROP-IN COUNSELING HOURS:** Your school counseling center will likely offer some access to counselors without an appointment (for urgent care). Find out the hours, location, and contact information.

- **APPOINTMENTS:** Your counseling center will probably accept scheduled appointments. Some schools offer a limited number of counseling sessions free of charge. Find out the number of counseling sessions your school offers, and whether this is for your entire time in college or per year.

- **SUPPORT GROUPS:** In addition to counseling, your school might offer support groups on campus or suggest support groups off campus for a variety of people and mental health needs. (A discussion about support groups in your college town can be found in chapter 9.)

- **REFERRALS TO OFF-CAMPUS PROVIDERS:** Your school's mental health professionals might refer you for additional care with a private physician or therapist.

Finding Off-Campus Counseling Services

You may might have additional mental health needs that your campus counseling services are unable to provide or need more counseling hours than your school provides to each student. These might include long-term formal psychological or psychiatric care; neurological evaluations; inpatient or outpatient treatment programs; or specialized treatment programs or support groups for alcohol or drug addiction or disordered eating. Many of these resources are readily available in the surrounding community.

Your campus health or counseling center clinician should be able to arrange a referral if you already know what type of care or services you need. In addition to the support groups that might be offered on your campus, others can be found in the local community. Regardless of whether you see a therapist on campus, join a support group, or see an off-campus provider, it is important that you view your sessions as a place where learning and growth can take place.

QUESTIONING WHETHER YOU'RE READY TO START COLLEGE DUE TO A HEALTH CONDITION OR UNFORESEEN CIRCUMSTANCE

Feeling nervous about this big transition in your life is expected. According to experts, moving from home to college is one of the biggest stressors young adults face. So if you find yourself worried, give yourself care, not judgment. If you feel like you're alone and your high school friends seem to be handling the countdown to college better than you are, remember that our public faces can be different from our internal lives. Just look at anyone's social media feed for proof.

Although some stress during this transitional time in your life is expected and won't prevent you from taking this big step, for some students, the stress of transition can be too much. Extreme stress or pain can exacerbate an existing physical or mental health condition. An event that could not be predicted, such as an illness, injury, family crisis, or the diagnosis of a chronic health condition, might emerge before you leave for school.

If any of these situations applies to you, now is a good time to reflect on how you are doing. Has the change in your life made it harder for you to do the things you normally do? Has it become more challenging for you to spend time with people? Most important, have your feelings about leaving for college been altered? If the answer to any of these questions is yes, that could be a sign that you're not simply experiencing normal stress—you could be in *distress*.

If you question whether you're ready to transition to college at this time, speak with your family, healthcare providers, and other trusted people in your life (such as a clergy member, coach, or mentor) about the possibility of deferring your admission for a semester until you feel that you have better control of your feelings and/or symptoms. Waiting a bit before starting college might seem like a failure to you, as you've been working toward college for so long and are so close to getting there. However, if you really aren't ready at this point, making this decision could help you avoid needing to leave during the school year, or your first semester turning into a negative or unhealthy experience. If deferring your admission is what you believe is right for you, know that this decision is not one of weakness, but instead shows maturity and strength. And it is not one you have to make alone. Talk to the people you trust the most.

PRO-TIP

If you are under eighteen, have a conversation with your parent(s) about getting permission for nonemergency medical care.

HEALTH COVERAGE AND INSURANCE

Most people don't buy healthcare—such as annual checkups, tests, and treatment for illnesses and injuries—directly. Instead, they use health insurance to cover fees for these and other types of healthcare. Their insurance plan pays healthcare providers most of the cost of care.

What Are the Different Types of Health Insurance?

There are several types of health insurance.

- **PRIVATE HEALTH INSURANCE:** Most Americans who are insured have plans with private insurance companies.

    - **EMPLOYER PROVIDED:** The majority of Americans use the health insurance plans provided by their (or a family member's) employer. This is often called employer-provided healthcare, but the employer usually doesn't pay for the entire plan. The employee contributes half or more of the fees (called "premiums") for this insurance.

- **EXCHANGES:** People can also buy private health insurance without going through an employer. Some do this through state or federal healthcare marketplaces, or "exchanges." These are government-run services that help people shop for and enroll in health insurance plans. Many people who buy their insurance this way are eligible for financial assistance with their premiums. Learn more at www.healthcare.gov.

- **GOVERNMENT HEALTH PLANS:** There are many kinds of government health plans, including Medicaid, which provides healthcare for many low-income people and people with disabilities; Medicare, which covers people over sixty-five and some younger people with disabilities; the Children's Health Insurance Program; and plans for veterans, military service members and their families (some government insurance programs have options that use private companies).

- **COLLEGE HEALTH PLANS:** As explained on the following pages, many colleges and universities offer their own insurance plans. Some college health insurance plans work with private insurance companies. Other colleges "self-insure," meaning that the school acts like its own insurance company.

Your School's Rules About Health Insurance

Most colleges and universities require students to have some form of health insurance. School policies about health insurance vary. Your school might:

- Require you to prove that you have insurance, but not restrict you to a particular type of plan.

- Require you to enroll in the university health plan regardless of whether you have other insurance.

- Enroll all students in the college plan automatically, but let students opt out if they demonstrate they have other insurance.

- Charge a "health fee" that covers care at the campus health center.

In passing during office hours, a student said she was stressed out because she hadn't been running, something she did to relieve stress. When asked why, she said that she had hurt her knee and the urgent care said she needed to see an orthopedist. She said she couldn't do that until she went back to her home state two months later because she was on out-of-state insurance. She didn't know that it was possible for her to see an "out-of-network" provider. When she learned that, she called the number on her insurance card for information.

—COLLEGE PROFESSOR

How Insurance Works

Some features of health insurance plans are similar regardless of what kind of plan you have—your school's health plan, your family's or employer's plan, a program for military families or veterans, or another government health plan.

Features common to most health insurance:

- **COPAYS:** When you visit a doctor, even one who participates in your insurance, you might be charged a fee called a copay. Find out in advance what the copay is for the school health plan. Note: The copay for a checkup might be different than for a visit to a specialist, such as an orthopedist or psychiatrist.

- **PARTICIPATING PROVIDERS:** Not all healthcare providers accept every kind of insurance. Your health insurance plan's website will have names of providers, including specialists, in your area who accept your insurance. Check the list before making an appointment. If a doctor recommends you see a specialist, check the website and find out whether the recommended physicians participate in your plan.

- **OUT-OF-NETWORK PROVIDERS:** If you see a doctor outside your insurance network, most insurance plans will pay some portion of that doctor's fees. You might find that you have to visit a doctor who does not accept your school's coverage, for example; find out how much of the cost of seeing an out-of-network provider your school plan will pay. Then talk to your parents or guardians about how they want you to pay for it. Will you have access to a credit card for this purpose?

- **PRESCRIPTION COVERAGE:** Many insurance plans cover prescription medications.

  - Many plans will have prescription copays, much like for medical appointments. Find out your prescription copay for each prescription medication you take.
  - Often, insurance will cover the cost of "generic" drugs but not brand-name drugs. An example of a brand-name drug that many students use is Advil, a pain reliever that doesn't require a prescription. The generic name for this drug is ibuprofen. Many prescription drugs have generic versions, too. Before you leave for college, find out whether the school's health insurance covers the cost of brand-name drugs or only generic alternatives, and whether your doctor approves of your using the generic version (most of the time, they do).
  - Some plans require you to use a mail-order pharmacy service for long-term prescriptions. You will need to find out whether this is the case with your prescription plan.

- **RESPONSIBLE PARTY FOR NONCOVERED EXPENSES:** When you fill out forms at a new doctor's office, they will ask you to identify the party who is responsible for any expenses that are not covered by insurance. You will need to clarify with your parents or guardians who that person will be. If different individuals share the responsibility for your expenses, make sure you know who is responsible for the expenses your plan does not cover, including copays.

There might be some differences between your college plan or other plans when it comes to on-campus healthcare:

  - **SCHOOL HEALTH PLANS:** Often, students who are enrolled in the school health plan have to go to the school health center before seeking a specialist or outside doctor (except in an emergency). Your school's health plan website and plan documents will explain whether you need to do so. Familiarize yourself with the required procedures for checkups, visits for illness, and specialists (such as an orthopedist for a sports injury)

- **OTHER HEALTH PLANS:** Your campus health center might not accept outside insurance other than in emergencies. Check the health center's website to find out whether they accept your plan.

DO BEFORE YOU GO

Learn about your insurance plan and add the following essential information to your smartphone (and browser, if applicable). (See "Make Your Smartphone Smarter" on page 277 and "Boost Your Browser" on page 278 for checklists of information you should store.)

- Insurance plan information
  - Insurance plan name and phone number.
  - ID# (you might also want to scan a copy of your insurance card and save it on your phone and in your computer)
  - Insurance plan website address
  - Whether the plan covers prescriptions
  - Prescription plan information (if it's a separate plan)
- There are smartphone apps designed to help you manage information about your healthcare, including insurance, prescriptions, provider contacts, health history, and current symptoms. Some insurers provide or recommend such an app. Ask your insurer about them. Some colleges and universities also offer or recommend health apps. Your college health center or insurance plan will know more. Other apps are available through the App Store and Google Play. You might want to research these apps and decide whether to use one.

DISCUSS BEFORE YOU GO

Which health insurance plan will you enroll in? If your school lets you choose from among different insurance options, it's helpful to consider the following questions when you and your family make your decision:

- How much will it cost to receive care from providers near your school?

- Does your scholarship require you to adopt the student health plan?

- If you are an international student, are you required to enroll in the campus health insurance plan?

- How does the premium or annual fee for the school plan compare to the premiums for your family's plan?

- Does the school health plan cover you year-round?

- Does the school health plan cover providers near your home (for breaks and summer) and is this considered in network or out of network?

- If the campus health center doesn't take your family's health plan, are there other healthcare options, such as hospitals and clinics, close by?

- Does your family's health insurance plan require you to get a referral from your healthcare provider before you can see a specialist?

- Is the premium the same regardless of how many children in your family are covered?

★★★

Remember that your college orientation provides you more time to learn specifics about your campus health, including where the offices are located and the hours they are open for scheduled appointments and emergencies. But this isn't enough. The well-prepared high school graduate should arrive on campus ready to *transition* toward managing their own health as a young adult. This includes knowing what to pack, when and where to seek care, and how to pay for it. Families at home and resources on your new campus are there to partner with you in this transition.

11

YOU ARE YOUR OWN SAFETY NET: STAYING PROTECTED IN COLLEGE

Campus safety is an extremely important issue for parents, students, and campus administrators. Campus safety officials are committed professionals who are engaged with their students, faculty, and staff to ensure their communities are safe places where students can learn and grow.

—UNIVERSITY PUBLIC SAFETY OFFICER

CAMPUS SAFETY

Let's face it—someone else was most likely looking out for your safety when you were in high school. Your school itself probably had a sign-in for visitors, locked doors, or some other way to try to keep students out of harm's way. You were also probably expected to check in with a parent or other family member when you were away from home so they could keep track of your whereabouts. Perhaps you had a curfew or were required to call or text to ask for permission to go somewhere, or at least inform someone where you were.

College, of course, is very different. Student safety is a priority for every college, and you can rest assured that most campuses are very safe environments. However, with so many people living in such close proximity, even the safest campuses experience their share of crimes, burglaries, and assaults every year. While you are adjusting to other adulting tasks, don't forget to prepare yourself with information to help you live as safely as possible while you're away at school.

DO BEFORE YOU GO

Prepare to Be the Sole Person Responsible for Your Own Safety and Well-Being in College

Stay alert and aware of your surroundings:

- If you are walking alone, even in your familiar home neighborhood, practice using headphones in only one ear.
- If you are at a party, practice keeping any open drink with you at all times to make sure that nothing is added to it.

Practice bystander intervention by *trusting your instincts*:

- If you notice something that doesn't feel right, it probably isn't.
- Step up to report feeling uncomfortable or unsafe, or to help others in similar situations.

Although your new roommate(s) and friends will look out for you and your school will have police or safety officers trained to help avoid risks for students on your campus, *you* will be the person most responsible for your own safety in college. Therefore, there are some things you should begin to think about before you head off to your new campus.

Your preparation involves the following:

- What you can do to prepare to be as safe as possible in college
- Emergency preparedness

- Public safety and sexual assault resources on your campus and in your college town
- Your legal rights to protection

Avoid walking on campus by yourself; this is especially important at night. It's easy to become so comfortable on campus that you let your guard down, but bringing a friend (or multiple friends) along with you when you're going to the gym or the library is always a smart idea.
—COLLEGE STUDENT

Staying Safe When You're Walking

You Shouldn't:
- Walk alone on campus at night or in an unfamiliar area.
- Try new paths after dark, even if they are shortcuts.
- Show confusion, even if you are lost.

You Should:
- Use the buddy system or call your campus safety escort service.
- Stick to routes which are familiar, even if they take a little longer.
- Walk with confidence, even if you are unsure exactly where you are going.

Every campus has a security office or police department. Part of your tuition funds it, so make the most of this resource by learning what services it offers to students.

KNOW BEFORE YOU GO

Don't wait until you get to campus to learn what your school provides. Check out your school's public safety website in advance.

Although each campus safety department offers different services based on funding and geography, the majority have the following:

- **CAMPUS SAFETY ESCORT SERVICES** are among the most-used security services on college campuses. Your school might hire campus police officers, security officers, student employees in work-study programs, or a combination of these people to serve as escorts by shuttle, car, or on foot. Wherever you need to go, whether it is to the library late at night for a study group, or from a party back to your residence hall, your campus' escort service will ensure that you are not traveling alone. Having the safety escort service phone number in your phone is a smart idea.

Campus escort services were a huge relief to me as a freshman. Whether I was studying late at the library or just hanging out with friends on the other side of campus, I knew that I had a resource to get back to my room. Even just knowing that this was a service made me feel safe and comfortable on campus.

—COLLEGE STUDENT

- **BLUE LIGHT/EMERGENCY PHONE STATIONS** are placed around most campuses for students, employees, and visitors to use when they need any type of assistance. Once the call button is pressed, the phone system instantly connects the person to the campus police department dispatcher.

- Almost every college student carries a cell phone with them, and this is important, not just to connect to friends and family, but also for your safety. Make sure to sign up for campus alert text messages and download the safety apps that your school suggests. Turning on the location services on your laptop and cell phone (such as the "find my phone" feature) will help campus police find you or your technology quickly in an emergency.

  - **CAMPUS ALERTS:** Most colleges use a campus alert system as the emergency messaging platform that enables administrators to send real-time emergency messaging by text or voice mail to students, faculty, and staff. Some colleges also encourage parents of students to enroll. These messages include information about campus lockdowns, severe weather, or building evacuation procedures.

  - **SAFETY APPS:** The heightened concern about campus security nationwide combined with the technical abilities of mobile devices are driving the demand for campus safety apps such as CampusSafe, Rave Guardian, Circle of 6, and EmergenSee. Many students feel more comfortable texting than reporting suspicious behavior by phone, and most of these apps use GPS so that students can send tips and photos to university police.

DO BEFORE YOU GO

- Find the phone numbers for your campus police department and safety escort service on their websites and program them into your cell phone.

- Sign up for your college alert system, which provides immediate texts regarding campus-wide safety and weather alerts.

- Download a safety app that your college suggests.

- Save the phone numbers of family/friends whom you might reach out to in an emergency.

Your Campus' Crime Data Is Readily Available to You

The more you know about the crime in your local area, the better you can prevent similar incidents from happening to you. Several websites offer a thorough overview of your new city's crime rates, organized by type of offense and specific locations where the crimes occurred. A site like City-Data.com will help you learn more about the crime within a particular city.

In addition to the crime statistics published about your new city, The Jeanne Clery Disclosure of Campus Security Policy and Campus Crime Statistics Act (known as the Clery Act) is a federal statute requiring colleges and universities participating in federal financial aid programs to maintain and disclose campus crime statistics and security information. US Department of Education regulations require every college or university in the United States to:

- Collect, classify, and count crime reports and crime statistics.

- Issue campus alerts to provide the campus community with information necessary to make informed decisions about their health, safety, and any threat.

- Provide educational programs and campaigns to promote awareness of dating violence, domestic violence, sexual assault, and stalking.

- Disclose their procedures for institutional disciplinary action in cases of dating violence, domestic violence, sexual assault, and stalking in their published annual security report.

- Disclose their crime statistics by type, location, and year.

- Keep a daily crime log of alleged criminal incidents on your campus that is open to the public.

If you would like to see any of this information, simply go to your school's campus safety website or the US Department of Education's campus safety website, ope.ed.gov/campussafety.

YOUR PERSONAL SAFETY AND EMERGENCY PREPAREDNESS

Although you can't predict when emergencies will happen (that's what makes them emergencies), you *can* take steps to be safer and better prepared.

What to Purchase and What to Do for College Safety

Purchasing a few safety supplies can help you feel more protected in your new environment. When you are purchasing your bedding and other accessories for your residence hall, buy some safety-related items as well, some for your room and some to carry with you in your backpack or purse at all times.

> ### KNOW BEFORE YOU GO
>
> Check if your school provides a locking safe in your residence hall room. If not, consider purchasing a portable safe for storing your technology, medications, and other valuables such as cash, a passport, or jewelry when you're away from your room.
>
> Chain stores like Target and Bed Bath & Beyond carry small dorm safes at reasonable prices.

Campus police across the United States suggest that all students come to college prepared to be advocates for their own safety.

Easy Things You Can Do to Keep Your Possessions Safe

You Shouldn't:

- Leave your residence hall room empty and unlocked.
- Leave your laptop out in the library if you need to step away from studying.
- Leave valuables out in the open in your residence hall room.

You Should:

- Lock your door, even if you will be gone for a few minutes.
- Ask someone you know and trust to watch your laptop or take it with you.
- Put electronics in a drawer and lock up valuables such as passports and jewelry.

DO BEFORE YOU GO

- Attach a whistle to the keychain or lanyard that you will use in college
- Purchase a small pepper spray or mace (if permitted on campus and in the state) to carry in your purse or backpack.
- Make sure you have a flashlight (and extra batteries) in your room for power outages.
- Keep a small phone charger and an external battery with a charging cord with you so that you can recharge if the power goes out or you don't have access to an outlet.
- Have your residence hall address memorized.
- Take photos of the serial numbers of your important technology. This will aid the public safety officers if those items are ever lost or stolen.

Maintain Privacy on Social Media

Social media is a great platform for connecting with friends and family worldwide or sharing updates about your life. However, with everything you post, stay aware of who else could be viewing your profile. Campus safety experts suggest that you avoid geotagging your photos, which reveals your location to strangers, and that you don't publicly announce when you're home alone or that you're leaving your residence hall alone.

DO BEFORE YOU GO

- Turn off geotagging.
- Make your social media accounts private.
- Use your GPS to find popular, highly trafficked routes to get around your new city or town.

Learn How to Defend Yourself

If you are not familiar with or comfortable protecting yourself physically, consider taking a self-defense class before moving to college; learning to protect yourself physically is quite empowering. Many states offer free or inexpensive self-defense classes such as R.A.D. (Rape Aggression Defense) or similar self-defense education programs. Martial arts studios, local college gyms, fitness centers, and police stations are other places to get some basic instruction. Ask a friend or family member to join you if you are uncomfortable taking a class alone. Check out your college police department as well; many offer free self-defense training for students, which you can sign up for once you're on campus.

Sexual Assault on College Campuses

Sexual assault, also called sexual violence or sexual abuse, is any type of sexual activity or contact that happens *without your consent*. It can include contact activities, such as rape or unwanted touching, and non-contact activities, such as someone exposing themselves to you or forcing you to look at sexual images. The most important thing to know is that if you believe you were assaulted, it is *not* your fault. College campuses can offer a false sense of security—a feeling that everyone knows each other and watches out for one another. Know that there are perpetrators who take advantage of this feeling of safety to commit sexual assault.

Legal definitions of sexual assault and other crimes of sexual violence vary among states. It is important to know what these definitions entail in the state or city where your college is located *and* specifically on your campus. Your school's Title IX office will have this information.

KNOW BEFORE YOU GO

- Find the legal definition of sexual assault as it is defined by your college and by the state in which your college is located.
- Search online to find and familiarize yourself with information about your school's resources for sexual assault, such as the campus health center, campus police station, sexual assault services, and campus security escorts.

DISCUSS BEFORE YOU GO

Spend some time with your family discussing backup plans for uncomfortable and potentially dangerous situations you might encounter in college. Here are some discussion prompts:

- What should you do if you are unable to use an ATM or credit card due to a power outage?
- What does your family expect of you in terms of public transportation usage and walking alone in your new city?
- Who will be your local contact in an emergency situation if you will be living far from home?
- What are the expectations of you if you will be away from campus overnight?

★★★

In this chapter, we've discussed what you can do to prepare yourself for a safe transition to campus living and presented tips you can use to protect yourself and your possessions. We suggest that you take the safety smarts from this chapter and apply them to the wider community. (In chapter 20, you will learn about your new college town, its geography, and what it has to offer you.)

PART IV

THE RESIDENT EXPERTS

In this section, we'll introduce you to the resident experts on your campus who will guide you through your college experience. This includes both staff, administrators, and the college faculty (professors). You'll read about the different roles filled by these two groups of individuals and learn how their jobs compare to the staff and teachers at your high school. We'll explain the positions of the top administrators at your college or university, and then dive into the impact of the student-facing staff, who you'll interact with on a weekly (if not daily) basis.

Next, we'll talk about your college professors and learn about their differing expertise, career paths, research and professional work, teaching responsibilities, and level of student interaction. You'll also learn a little bit about graduate teaching assistants and undergraduate peer leaders and what they do (and shouldn't do) in the college classroom. We'll explain the importance of maintaining a professional relationship with both groups of individuals on your campus. Finally, you'll see how both faculty and staff contribute to mentoring, serving, and teaching students, inside and outside the classroom.

KEY PLAYERS ON CAMPUS:
STAFF AND ADMINISTRATORS

The staff who work on your campus will contribute to the success of your college experience. Since most high school organizational charts look completely different than those of a college or university campus, we'll start with an explanation of the differences between faculty and staff.

QUESTIONS	FACULTY	STAFF
What do they do?	Teach, conduct research, and engage in service; support students	Serve in their assigned specialized roles; function as employees of an organization; support students
What hours do they work?	Irregular, but usually required to hold mandatory office hours	Usually regular business hours, depending on position
What positions are included?	Range: full professors, associate professors, assistant professors, lecturers, researchers, and fellows	Range: from administrative support to deans, psychologists, cleaning service workers, the registrar, department directors, and the school president
What is their educational background?	Usually hold the highest degree (doctorate or master's) in their field, as per criteria set by the institution	Usually a graduate-level degree at all levels in varied academic specialty areas

THE ADMINISTRATION

At a higher education institution, the word *staff* has a very broad meaning, as it is a collective term that refers to all the employees working on (and sometimes off) campus. A college staff consists of individuals with different educational and professional expertise who either work directly with students, families, and alumni, or serve the school as an institution. As a college student, especially one at a large college or university, you might not interact all that much with the senior-level administrative staff at your school. However, as a college student, you should still understand what the most senior-ranking people on your campus actually do.

- Your **COLLEGE PRESIDENT** or **CHANCELLOR** is the leader of the school and is responsible for the organization and administration of it, both on and off campus. Presidents are expected to fund-raise for their college or university, raise the profile of their school with public appearances, recommend changes in personnel and personnel policies, submit an annual budget and administer the budget approved by the board of trustees, direct the development of new buildings on campus, and meet with faculty, staff, and students to address their concerns.

- Your PROVOST is the chief academic officer at your school and is responsible for the creation and implementation of the academic priorities and for the allocation of resources that will support those priorities. The provost collaborates with the president in setting overall academic priorities for the school and ensuring that top faculty are recruited. Your provost works closely with the academic deans, department heads, student services professionals, faculty, and staff to provide quality educational programs for students at all levels.

- Your DEAN OF STUDENTS plans and directs university activities related to student services and campus life. Depending on the structure of your school, this person might oversee the office of admissions, counseling services, Greek life, orientation, international student programming, health services, financial aid, housing, and social programs for students. The Office of the Dean of Students is generally responsible for serving as a point of information and referral for students, responding to their needs, and handling discipline-related procedures.

- Your ACADEMIC DEAN governs their individual school and serves as the chief representative of the school to the rest of the college or university. Academic deans manage the budget for their school and coordinate its curriculum development. They also evaluate their department chairs, directors, faculty, and staff in teaching, research, and service and provide recommendations to the provost.

KNOW BEFORE YOU GO

Look up the name and bios of your college president, provost, dean of students, the academic dean of your college (based on what major you are expecting to declare), and the student government president so you know who governs your school and is ultimately responsible for the decisions made about your college experience.

At most medium and large schools, you're not likely to meet one-on-one with these college administrators unless you serve in a specialized role such as a student trustee, in student government, or on a campus-wide committee. However, some top administrators will hold community forums for students, faculty, and staff to share concerns, such as financial aid or changes to the core curriculum. Attending a few of these events will be worthwhile to you as a first-year student, especially when the topic at hand is something that will affect you directly.

There are some schools (usually the smaller ones) where the top administrators are not only seen regularly on campus, but also make a point of interacting with the students in their residence halls, during sporting events, or in the dining hall. If this opportunity is part of your school's culture, we encourage you to take full advantage of events with names like "Bagels with the Provost" or "Tea with the President."

STUDENT-FACING STAFF

Undergraduate students do interact frequently with staff members on campus in order to obtain critical information about many things that affect their daily lives, including housing, tutoring, career services, student organizations, planning your courses, and dining. You may also want or need support for your mind and body and will rely on the staff who provide health and/or wellness services.

There are more than enough resources on campus that exist to make your time as a college student much easier. Need a job on campus? Visit the career center and see the available options for you. Feeling overwhelmed with the changes that you're going through? Making an appointment at the counseling center and finding mentors can help. Having difficulty writing a long research paper? Reach out to your professor, then stop by the writing center or the Academic Support Center to seek help. Need help planning your academic career? Talk to your academic adviser. There are

various resources that will help you if you are struggling in any class in addition to reaching out to your professor.

—COLLEGE STUDENT

Perhaps it is the staff member who sits behind the reference desk in the library and helps you find a resource for a paper, or the campus police officer who gives you an escort back to your room late at night. Possibly it is the academic adviser who works with you to plan your course schedule, or the financial aid officer who helps you with a loan application. Maybe it is the psychologist who runs a support group you attend, or the coordinator who plans the diversity programming on your campus. Similar to the relationships that you can build with your professors, you have an opportunity to develop mentoring relationships with campus staff members that may last your entire four years if you seize the opportunity.

The important thing to remember is this: Librarians want to help you. It is not an inconvenience or a bother to approach a librarian. Helping students is what we love about our jobs!

—COLLEGE LIBRARIAN

Unlike in high school, when your parents or other family members may have been involved in conversations with school staff such as counselors and principals on your behalf, in college you will engage directly with staff on your own. You might approach a staff member about roommate conflicts, financial aid forms, disability support, or your academic course load. There are a few exceptions. For example, if you are experiencing a health crisis or other emergency, or if there is a fear that you are a danger to yourself or others, your college staff and administrators may contact your family directly. But overwhelmingly, it's on *you* to work with staff to ask questions, solve problems, and advance your goals.

This includes times when you are dissatisfied with the way your school is handling an issue. Your family can be a great source of *guidance* on a problem you might be encountering, but they should act to support you, not step in to solve it. College staff are professionals who are trained to work with young adults. They will usually know how to problem-solve with you (and chances are, you're not the first student to approach them with the same challenges).

Engaging Professionally with Staff

Many first-year college students develop early and close relationships with student-facing staff, especially those in academic advising, housing, and student activities. However, it's important to remember that you are building adult, professional relationships with these individuals in a college setting. As comfortable as you feel approaching these staff members, remember that they are in a professional work environment, and they are not your peers. Unsure what to call a staff member? Start by looking up their bio online and assume you should use the most formal title based on what you read.

Staff members (including those behind the scenes, such as the service workers who cook your food or clean your residence hall and classrooms) are there to help build your college experience. However, with the exception of some staff members who live on campus, most go home at the end of the day. They do things after work like cook dinner, pick up their kids, go to the gym, and even take evening classes. Keep this in mind when you are scheduling a meeting with a member of your college staff or sending an email after work hours (see "Writing a Professional Email" in chapter 5). Reach out to those staff members by email before you get to campus and introduce yourself. Having a person waiting to support you on campus is a great idea for anyone.

DISCUSS BEFORE YOU GO

- Have a conversation with your family about which staff members on your campus you might benefit from knowing.
- Talk about the leading role you plan to take in engaging with the staff who support your college experience. If you vent to your parents about a residence life issue, does that mean you want them to reach out to professional staff or advise you on how to handle it?

A Note on "Mandated Reporters"

In your time as a college student, you will likely build productive, trusting relationships with one or more staff members or professors. What you share with faculty and staff is not always confidential, however. When you disclose information about sexual assault, harassment, stalking, and other issues covered by Title IX of the Education Amendments Act, many faculty and staff are required to report this to the administration (see chapter 11 for more information).

Take advantage of the professionals who are specially trained to work with college students on your campus; remember that these staff are the experts in many of your experiences outside the classroom. Make the time to introduce yourself to other college staff members when you are *not* asking them for help. Say hello to the administrative assistants in your professors' departments—don't just zoom by their desks on your way to office hours. You'll likely find that college staff become part of your support network, and getting to know them can also help make your college feel like a community.

In the next chapter, you'll learn about the people who will play the largest role in your college academic experience: the professors.

13

NOT SO SCARY AFTER ALL:
PROFESSORS

PRO-TIP

**Like Santa, your professor knows when you are sleeping. She
knows when you're awake. And when you've done the reading.
And when you're shopping for shoes on your smartphone during
class. Think about it.**

In chapters 4 and 5, you learned about college-level academic expectations and the habits and practices of successful students. In this chapter, we'll talk about the people who will be your guides through college academics: your professors.

In many ways, college professors' backgrounds, expectations, and ways of doing things are not like those of anyone you've known. Not only are they completely new to you, they are authority figures who will play a formal role in your future. Regardless of whether a professor is the chair of your academic major department or teaches an interesting class you took on a lark, you will need to establish a professional, respectful, and productive relationship with them.

COLLEGE PROFESSORS VS. HIGH SCHOOL TEACHERS

You've been in school most of your life, and unless you were exclusively homeschooled, you're used to having a crop of new teachers every year or even every semester. So what will be familiar and what will be different?

Like your high school teachers, your professors want students to show respect and demonstrate responsibility, intellectual curiosity, and pride in their work. Like your high school teachers, your professors are busy—their time in the classroom represents a fraction of their time at work. Like your high school teachers, your professors are older than you. They have chosen to build a career in education and care about both their subject matter and their students.

However, their backgrounds, expectations, and approaches are likely to be very different.

Education and Training	
HIGH SCHOOL TEACHER	COLLEGE PROFESSOR
• Primarily focuses on teaching	• Might conduct research in addition to teaching
• Studied to become a teacher	• Studied to become a subject-matter expert
	• Might have taken one course about teaching as a part of their doctoral program

• Often required to teach a school-approved curriculum (or one geared toward a test such as the AP)	• Often designs her or his courses from scratch (particularly advanced courses; but you might find that most sections of intro to calculus at your school are similar)
• Likely to come from the region or even the city where the school is and where you grew up	• Most likely did not come from the city or state where your university is located (many even hail from other countries)
• Usually has earned a master's degree, often in education	• Usually has earned a doctorate in the field, or another advanced degree such as a law degree

WHO ARE PROFESSORS?

According to the National Center for Education Statistics (www.nces .ed.gov), there were 1.6 million faculty at degree-granting postsecondary institutions in 2015. About half of these professors are full-time and half are part-time. If your professor teaches part-time, you should be aware that they are only on campus certain days of the week, and plan accordingly.

Like your high school teachers, your professors are ten to fifty (or more) years older than you. The differences between your generation and your professors' generations are most apparent in your relationships with technology, information, and communication. Your professors have been trained in academic research methods, which you can also expect to learn in college. But even before their graduate studies, your professors most likely did the bulk of their research using books and other printed texts—not search engines.

While you might communicate with your friends mostly by text, your professors will expect you to check your school email at least daily and will typically not give you their cell numbers. You should not plan to get instant responses from them; email responses will take longer.

Finally, professors' social media experiences will likely be different from yours. Many people, especially students, share extensive personal information on social media. Although professors care about their students' well-being and success, they are not your peers. Remember— this is a professional relationship, and your college is your professor's workplace.

WHAT DO PROFESSORS THINK (AND DOES IT MATTER)?

Whether it be participating in class or visiting a professor's office hours, don't be afraid to use your voice. In most discussion-based classes, professors don't care if you agree with their opinions or not; rather, they want you to form your own opinion/argument and articulate it well.

—COLLEGE STUDENT

When you told your friends and family you planned to go to college, it's possible you were warned about being "indoctrinated" by professors with a political agenda. In our politically polarized environment, colleges and universities—and particularly the professors who teach in them—are often targets of criticism for promoting a narrow set of ideas or punishing students who disagree.

Fortunately, this is overwhelmingly not the case. Your grades in college will reflect the work you put in and the extent to which you develop academic skills such as information literacy, critical thinking, and professionalism.

The purpose of higher education is to train students to ask and answer tough questions and to solve challenging problems—from complex mathematical equations to the question of whether to raise the minimum wage.

Your professor *is* looking for a certain kind of answer—a well-reasoned one supported by evidence. In first-year courses, the evidence you use to support your claims will most likely come from assigned readings in the course. As you progress through college, you will conduct more original research and be responsible for evaluating your sources.

But what if you *do* disagree with your professor? College professors want to hear your thoughts, even if those thoughts differ from their own; the ability to think critically is what college is all about. However, thinking critically does not mean debating the professor's beliefs or what you *think* the professor believes; students' assumptions about professors' politics are almost always irrelevant to the learning process. Over your time in college, you'll learn to challenge the material presented—and your professors' views of it—by introducing evidence to support alternative views. Your professors' and teaching assistants' office hours are a great time to ask questions that challenge what you're learning in class.

WHEN YOU'RE THERE

Asking questions is one of the hallmarks of critical thinking. Great students ask professors to recommend readings that go deeper into a topic or present alternative theories.

PRO-TIP

We see lots of smart students every year. The ones who show initiative, take responsibility, and are honest, reliable, and trustworthy build the best relationships with their professors.

YOUR RELATIONSHIP WITH PROFESSORS

Your relationship with each of your professors is also new; it's a relationship between two adults. Your professor is an authority figure, but unlike a parent or a high school teacher, he or she are not a caregiver or parental figure.

Getting Acquainted

You will find out who your professors are when you receive your course schedule. Take the time to learn something about them by visiting their profile page on your university's website. Where did they go to school? What kind of research do they conduct? Have they worked in government, the private sector, nonprofits, or at other universities? You might find you share some common ground or interests.

A WORD OF CAUTION ABOUT PROFESSOR RATING SITES

We recommend that you take reviews on these sites with a grain of salt. Unlike your university's own evaluation system, these pages often don't verify that the posters are even students; very few people post ratings, and students who are dissatisfied with the course (or their grades) are more likely to post than satisfied students, which can skew the results. They don't show how the majority or even a representative sample of a professor's students think of them.

Communicating

Rule #1: It's on the syllabus.
Rule #2: Seriously—it's on the syllabus.

It's important to develop a professional, productive relationship with your college professors. As a start, you should be aware that your professors are the first line of support in your academic work. You don't need to have a problem in class to look to your professors and TAs as a resource. You can look to them for guidance on how to succeed in your classes from day one.

It's Just the Two of You

HIGH SCHOOL TEACHER	COLLEGE PROFESSOR
• Might communicate with your parents or guardians in conferences or when problems arise	• Because of a law called the Family Educational Rights and Privacy Act (FERPA), professors can't communicate with your parents about your class performance. If serious problems arise, they might discuss issues with the college administration
• Will likely reach out to you if you are not doing the reading or performing up to your ability	• Is more likely to expect you to seek help or guidance on your own
• Acts *in loco parentis*, which means in the place of parents, during the school day	• Expects you to take care of yourself as an adult
• Sets up meetings with you before school, after school, during lunch, or during their free periods to answer questions and provide academic help	• Offers scheduled weekly office hours and might hold hours by appointment
• Expects you to call them Mr./Mrs./Ms. XX or by a first name, depending upon your school	• Should be called Professor XX (or Dr. XX, if they hold a PhD) unless they indicate otherwise

Going to office hours before you need help can build relationships with faculty, so if the scenario that you need help arises, the professor will already know who you are.

—COLLEGE STUDENT

For every hour your professors spend in the classroom, they spend many more hours preparing for class sessions, grading assignments, conducting research, holding office hours, serving on university committees, and advising students. Your professor is there to help, but you can't expect to get instant responses to emails or a same-day appointment for a meeting.

DO: Email your professor well in advance of the time you need an answer to a question and ask when they might be available.
DON'T: Send an email like this one: "Professor Jackson—I want to meet tomorrow at 4:30 to talk about my grade."

Professors appreciate when you show respect for their time. That means finding readily available information on your own and contacting your professor for expert help.

Go to your professors and TAs for:

- Clarification about course readings and concepts or assignment prompts
- Feedback on papers and advice on how to improve course performance
- Suggestions for further reading
- Deeper conversation about course concepts
- What you missed during excused absences (but do the reading first)
- Advice about further study in the discipline

They are *not* here to tell you:

- What's on the syllabus
- Where their offices are
- How to fix a technology issue

- What's in the reading if you haven't yet done it
- What you missed the day you had an unexcused absence, were late to class, or didn't do the reading

WHEN YOU'RE THERE

- Read your professors' bios and curriculum vitae (a résumé for academics) on your school's website and bookmark those pages in your browser.
- Find out where their offices are.
- Find out when they hold office hours and if those office hours are drop-in or by appointment.

DO BEFORE YOU GO

- Email your professors from your school email account to introduce yourself (see "Writing a Professional Email" in chapter 5).
- Make sure you've got your professors' email addresses in your contacts and that your spam filter isn't throwing them out.

DISCUSS BEFORE YOU GO

- Talk to your parents, teacher, or guidance counselor about the differences between high school and college. They can be a great source of advice about how to build professional relationships, ask questions of people in positions of authority, and even deal with personality issues. You can learn a lot from them, and this conversation will help build their confidence that you're ready for this new stage of your education.
- Discuss your new role as the point of contact with professors. You might want to discuss how you plan to handle situations such as your first disappointing grade or a conflict with a professor, including when and how you will inform them or seek their advice.

A NOTE ON TEACHING ASSISTANTS AND PEER LEADERS

In addition to your professors, your college courses might have a teaching assistant (TA) or a peer leader. TAs are usually graduate students who are pursuing a master's degree or PhD. They are often authorized to grade papers and exams, and generally hold their own office hours. In a large lecture course, there might be more than one TA. They can provide many of the same types of help as your professor. Your professor and TA will generally let you know whether there are some things (such as requests for extensions on papers) that only the professor can handle.

At some colleges, there are also undergraduate teaching assistants. They are usually students who have taken the course before and can offer support with learning the material, run small group discussions, organize activities, and/or help the professor with attendance, finding course readings, or other tasks. Undergraduate teaching assistants typically cannot grade papers or tests. However, they are a great resource to help you understand how to succeed in a class, get comfortable speaking up, and learn about school from a student's perspective.

Some classes, including classes with a co-curricular component (such as field trips or community service) and many first-year transition classes, have peer leaders. Peer leaders are undergraduates who help with everything from organizing trips to helping instructors facilitate discussions. Your peer leaders aren't professors, but they can teach you a lot about how to college.

Because TAs aren't professors and usually don't yet have their PhDs, you won't call them Professor XX or Dr. XX. Your individual graduate TAs will usually let you know how they want to be addressed—often by their first names. Until they tell you, use "Mr." or "Ms." and their last name. You'll address undergraduate TAs and peer leaders by their first name.

Now that you know more about professors and the people who help them teach your courses, remember to cultivate productive relationships with them. They are a resource for you in college, and if you lay the groundwork now, they can become mentors for many years after as you navigate your future career.

When you develop a solid network of supportive professors and others, great academic skills, and pursue your studies and jobs with professionalism, doors should open to you. As you learned in part III, taking care of yourself is essential to your success and happiness. Your financial health is also critical when it comes to your (bright) future. Having good credit shows your future employers and landlords that you're responsible. Keeping your costs down could enable you to take the job you truly want, even if it's not the one that pays the most. On the other hand, having bad credit or excessive debt can close doors to you. That sounds scary—especially now, when college and housing cost so much—but you can do it. In part V, you'll learn the basics of personal finance for college students and get some tools to make financially sound decisions.

PART V

MONEY TALK

When you started high school, your family and counselors most likely told you everything you did would go on your transcript and that colleges would see it all.

Now that you're heading for college, your financial condition—your debt, savings, credit history, expenses, and income—are like that transcript. Your decisions affect your quality of life in the present and your options in the future.

Preparing to handle your finances might sound like one of the scariest parts of going off to college. If you feel like you have no idea where to start, you're not alone. Studies show that most college students don't know basic facts about money, including budgeting, using credit, and savings. And most students didn't get *any* instruction on personal finance in high school.[v]

It's okay. This summer is a great time to start learning this adulting skill and to take some steps that will help you in your first year and beyond.

This part of the book will cover three topics: paying for college, understanding money, and budgeting. You'll have some simple and useful tasks to do this summer. One of them will be to track your spending for a week, so make sure you give yourself at least a week for this section of the book (and make sure it's a week you're not on vacation, since that wouldn't reflect your usual spending habits).

FAST FACT

Over two-thirds of students graduating from public colleges and three-quarters of students graduating from private nonprofit colleges have student loans.

14

YOU'RE NOT A LOAN:
PAYING FOR COLLEGE

By now you've most likely chosen your college and decided, with your family, how you will pay for it. This book is not intended to help you choose between schools or aid offers. However, if you *are* still deciding between aid offers, this chapter and chapter 15, which explains loans and credit, will still be useful for you. You can also go to the US Department of Education's federal student aid website (https://studentaid.ed.gov) for information about comparing student aid offers.

In this chapter, you will:

- Learn about the cost of attending college and calculate the net price for your college education.
- Take a look at the big picture of how you are paying and set up a meeting with your financial aid office.
- Get some information about work and work-study.

WORKING WITH YOUR FINANCIAL AID COUNSELOR

Your financial aid office is staffed by experts. They know college. They know *your* college. And they are trained to work with students. You should plan to meet with your financial aid staff regardless of whether you have a problem at the beginning of the year. Even if you do not have financial aid or loans, the financial aid office probably has resources for you, including information about merit-based awards and financial literacy materials.

KNOW BEFORE YOU GO

- Who is your assigned financial aid staff member?
- Where is their office?
- Do they have walk-in hours when you can meet them, or will you need an appointment?

UNDERSTANDING THE COST OF
ATTENDING YOUR COLLEGE

When you were applying to colleges, you most likely looked at websites explaining the total cost and showing how that cost breaks down into tuition, fees, room and board, books, insurance, and other costs. You might have worked with the financial aid office and admissions to put together a financial aid package. Even if you did, it is still worth looking at how you are paying for school, which will affect your decisions about work and budgeting.

If you did not apply for an aid package, whether that was because your family is paying for college or you received a full scholarship, it is still worth looking at your total cost in case you choose to transfer, your circumstances change, or you are deciding whether to incur debt for personal expenses not covered by your scholarship.

Total Cost

When we talk about the cost of college, we often call it "tuition." In fact, tuition—which is the price for instruction and programs—only makes up about 40 to 60 percent of your total cost of attending college. Your college's website will indicate the total cost of attending for

Tuition and Fees for Two Semesters		
	IN-STATE STUDENT	OUT-OF-STATE STUDENT
Tuition	$12,848	$35,216
University and Student Fees	$2,882	$2,882
On-Campus Housing Estimate	$7,028	$7,028
On-Campus Meal Plan Estimate	$5,846	$5,846
Subtotal Direct Costs	$28,604	$50,972
Waivable Fee: Health Insurance	$3,198	$3,198
Waivable Fee: PIRG Fee	$10	$10
Subtotal Direct Costs (plus Waivable Fees)	$31,812	$54,180[vi]

a year, broken down into categories of expenses. Here is an example from a state university.

Net Price

The "net" price of attending your college is the total cost of one year of college as a full-time undergraduate student, minus grants and scholarships (money that you don't have to pay back) that you receive.

It's important to understand that the net price is *not* the amount that you and your family actually pay out of your own pocket each year. It includes the amounts that you will pay for with student loans. Student loans are part of the cost of education even though you will not start paying them back until you graduate.

Colleges and universities are now required to have a net price calculator. You can also find one on the US Department of Education website at https://collegecost.ed.gov/netpricecenter.

DO BEFORE YOU GO

Calculate your net price per year.

HOW YOU'LL PAY FOR COLLEGE

It is helpful to know the vocabulary of paying for college.

Expected Family Contribution
(Including Loans)

When you apply to school and submit a FAFSA, your family will provide financial information that will be used to determine what your family can afford to pay toward your education. This is called the expected family contribution (EFC). As the cost of attending college has gotten steeper, more families find that they actually cannot afford to pay their EFC out of pocket (with money they already have). As a result, the family and/or student borrow money in the form of a loan (or loans) to pay for college.

When you think about your total family contribution to your college education, include money that your family will need to borrow.

DISCUSS BEFORE YOU GO

- How is your family paying for college?
- Is this going to remain the same after your first year?
- Will your scholarships or grants change?
- Will you continue to live on campus after your first year?
- What if your family's circumstances change?

Scholarships and Grants

People often use the words *scholarships* and *grants* interchangeably. While they share an important feature—you don't have to pay for them—they are not exactly the same.

Many of the most common grants are awarded based on need. The most common grant is the Pell Grant, which the federal government awards to students whose family income is below a certain level. State governments and schools also award grants. Some grants are awarded based on merit or on a combination of need and merit.

Most scholarships are based on merit, such as high grades or test scores or athletic ability. If your college or a private organization awarded you a merit scholarship, it's important for you to find out whether you have to meet certain requirements to keep the scholarship after your first year.

KNOW BEFORE YOU GO

If you have a merit scholarship, does your college require you to send your final high school transcripts to the financial aid office in order for the scholarship funds to be disbursed?

DO BEFORE YOU GO

- Contact your financial aid office and find out if they have all your necessary documents, including updated financial information and final transcripts.
- Send all the required information.

Loans

Most students borrow money for college. To learn more about how loans work, read chapter 15. For now, the important thing to understand is that when you and your family think about the cost of college, you should include loans. Not only will you or your family pay your loans back, but because of interest, you will pay back *more* than you borrowed—possibly twice as much, if you take ten years or more to repay the loans.

Work- Study

About 71 percent of students will work while they're in college. Chances are, at some point you'll have a job. But you'll also hear the term *work-study* on campus. It's a federal jobs program for eligible students, though not all schools participate. You must fill out a FAFSA to be eligible for work-study. Work-study isn't a grant or a scholarship, and the money doesn't go to the school—you receive it in a paycheck, just like any other job. What makes work-study different is that the government is funding it.

Important things to know about work-study:

- Some off-campus jobs can qualify for work-study. Your financial aid office will be able to help you find these jobs.

- Even if you qualify for a work-study job, your school does not have to offer you one on campus or guarantee that you find one off-campus.

- You need to reapply every year, and it's not guaranteed.

- Not all work-study jobs pay the same amount, but they all have to pay at least the federal minimum wage.

- The money you earn through work-study won't affect the amount of federal aid you receive. However, your federal award will specify a cap on your work-study earnings.

If you qualify for work-study jobs, you might have a choice between working on- or off-campus. In making this decision, consider the pros and cons. See chapter 19 for more information.

WHEN YOU'RE THERE

- Read all email and regular mail about grants, scholarships, and financial aid promptly—not having your aid in order can prevent you from registering for classes.
- Pay attention to campus news about new fees and tuition increases, and make your voice heard in the decision-making process.

- Mark your calendar with important financial aid deadlines.
- Keep an eye out for merit scholarships your school offers to students who meet certain criteria (such as high grades or community service).
- Keep the cost of college down (see chapter 16).

Whether you are paying for college on your own, with the help of family, through scholarships, or a combination of these, you need to take an active role in the process. This includes continuing to communicate with your family members about costs and contributions, maintaining your eligibility for merit scholarships, completing your FAFSA on time, and meeting with your financial aid officer.

The net price of college isn't the total cost of living in your time in college. Things like mobile phone service, personal items (like toiletries, clothes, and computers), and transportation cost a significant amount. But unlike your tuition, these are costs you can keep down. In chapters 15 and 16, you'll learn about how to maintain your financial health and keep costs down in college and beyond.

15

YOUR LIFE'S TRANSCRIPT: FINANCIAL LITERACY

For many students, college is the first time you will be managing your own money. Some of you already have bank accounts or credit cards of your own; others will use them for the first time. Regardless of whether you've used credit cards, debit cards, or banks before, it's important to learn about how to use them effectively once you're on your own to avoid mistakes that can cost you a lot of money.

Achieving basic financial literacy and following the best practices in this chapter will not only set you up for success—they will put you ahead of many people far older than yourself.

CREDIT HISTORY: YOUR FINANCIAL FINGERPRINTS

From the moment you make your first financial transaction—such as opening a bank account or applying for a credit card—you are building a record that will last a lifetime. This is called your credit history. Your credit history is your track record of incurring debt and paying debts and bills. It's like your social media activity—it never goes away, and it can affect your life.

How Can a Low Credit Score Affect Your Life?

- A landlord might conclude you can't be trusted to pay rent on time and reject your application to rent an apartment.

- A prospective employer might think you're unreliable (or have financial problems that pose a risk to them) and not hire you.

- When you apply for more credit, you could get turned down or be offered higher interest rates than someone with a better score.

Credit Reports: Your Life's Transcript

A number of private companies (the largest of which are TransUnion, Equifax, and Experian) gather data about your credit history—including your loans, credit cards, payment history, bank accounts, debts, and past applications for credit—and compile it into your credit report. Your credit report also includes your personal information, such as your address and Social Security number.

Current and potential employers, landlords, lenders, and insurers can see your credit report.

Credit Scores: Your Financial GPA

You might have heard the term *credit score*. If you have a credit history, you have a credit score ranging from 300 to 850. Businesses use this number to decide how risky it would be to lend you money, rent you an apartment, hire you, or sell you insurance. Your credit score is calculated from the contents of your credit reports, but does not appear on them.

Your credit score is based on:

- Your history of on-time payments: Paying on time improves your score.

- The amount of money you owe.

- The length of your credit history: The longer your credit history, the better.

- The number of recently opened accounts and recent inquiries into your credit report: If you open many accounts at once, you might see a drop in your score, but in general having multiple accounts does not negatively affect your score. And "soft" inquiries, like when you check your score online, do not count on your credit report.

- The types of credit you use: Later on in life, having a variety of types of credit is better, but as a college student without much income, you should not be trying to demonstrate that you can handle lots of types of credit right now.

PRO-TIP

Don't sign up for store credit cards just to get a discount on that day's purchase. Applying for the cards affects your credit score, and the more cards you need to keep track of, the more likely you are to miss a payment. Store credit cards tend to have very high interest rates, too, though they often offer a low initial rate. Falling behind on these payments can be very expensive.

You should check your credit score, preferably with all three of the largest credit reporting bureaus, at least once per year. Review your credit report in detail. Make sure all the accounts listed in the report are actually yours—if you don't recognize any, you will need to report that someone opened an account or accounts in your name. Look at negative marks such as late payments. If the information is wrong, you can use the credit bureau's dispute process to get it fixed. Your bank or money management app or program might have tools that allow you to check your credit report.

DO BEFORE YOU GO

Check your credit report and credit score on line (for free) at a site such as annualcreditreport.com.

BANKING

You don't have to use the bank that has a branch on your college campus. Shop around this summer.

Choosing a Bank Account: Find the Freebies

We know it sounds weird, but banks make you pay them to keep your money—even when you don't make any mistakes. When choosing an account, avoid or minimize these two common fees:

- A **minimum balance fee** (charged when your account balance drops below a certain level)
- A monthly or annual **maintenance fee**

Using Your Account: Avoiding Fees and Credit Problems by Keeping It Simple

There are two major things to avoid in using your bank account: late bill payments—which affect your credit score and, in the case of debt, increase the interest you have to pay—and spending more money than you have, which can result in large overdraft fees.

The following steps can help you minimize the risk of both late payments and overdrawing your account.

DIRECT DEPOSIT

If you have grants or scholarships that are disbursed to you instead of being sent directly to your school, you can have them deposited directly to your account. Check with your financial aid office about how to do this. You should also have your paychecks from all jobs deposited directly.

MOBILE APPS AND ONLINE BANKING

Most banks now have smartphone apps and online banking centers. These tools make paying bills, record keeping, and depositing money simple. When you open your account, download the bank's app and set up your online bill pay as soon as possible.

SCHEDULING BANKING TIME

Get in the habit of checking your money and managing your bills on a regular basis. The best way to do this is to make it a regular obligation— much like a class or a work shift. Select at least one day of the month for banking and put it on your calendar. During banking time, you should:

- Check your balance and be sure you can cover any payments that are scheduled to go out.

- Pay your credit card balance.

- Pay any other outstanding bills.

- Make sure your paychecks, money from family, and financial aid disbursements have been deposited.

- Look at the record of transactions and make sure none are fraudulent.

You should look at your account balance and activity more often, but the monthly banking time is a must.

It's important to keep track of everything you spend and any money you have coming in. Fortunately, online banking lets you track all your purchases and deposits. You still need to keep records, including student loan paperwork, because your records contain sensitive information.

DO BEFORE YOU GO

- Set up a checking account.
- Choose and apply for a credit card, if you plan to use one.
- Set up direct deposit for your grants and financial aid.
- Set up auto payments for any recurring cost for which you'll use the bank account or card.
- Register for online banking.
- Download your bank and credit card apps to your phone.
- Practice paying a bill online.
- Practice depositing a check using your bank's app.
- Choose a monthly banking time and put it in your calendar for every month of the year.

BORROWING: UNDERSTANDING CONSUMER DEBT

You will use your bank account to deposit and use the money you have. At times you'll also borrow money to make purchases and pay bills (such as your monthly mobile phone bill). Consumer financial products like credit cards can be convenient and very helpful in emergencies, but like many essential tools—such as cars and power drills—you need to get educated before you use them, and be careful when you do.

PRO-TIP

Treat your credit card like a gift card with less than your monthly budget remaining on it. Use it as a convenient way to spend what you have—not a way to spend more.

Debt is money you've spent that you never actually had. Debt costs money, and the longer you have it, the more money it costs. Because education has gotten so expensive, most college students won't have a choice about whether to go into debt.

But you *can* minimize your consumer debt—such as spending on credit cards and making purchases on payment plans. In chapter 16, you'll look at ways to limit your spending (a great way to avoid debt). Here you'll learn to manage your consumer debt and avoid typical problems.

Credit Card Interest

PRO-TIP

When you get an offer for a 0% interest credit card, check the conditions. This introductory rate will last for a short period and it's likely that if you miss even one payment, your rate will go up permanently.

Most credit cards give you one month after each purchase before your interest starts accruing. That's why it's very important to pay off your entire balance every month. After that, you start paying interest—and it piles up.

Your credit card charges interest at a standard rate called the annual percentage rate (APR). If you don't know your APR, call your credit card company or check online. Don't let the word *annual* fool you; your credit card interest grows *daily*. To understand how much your debt is growing each day, divide your APR by 365. If your APR is 19%, your daily interest is .052054%. It might not sound like a lot, but it adds up. If you owe $1,000 on a credit card with an APR of 19%, after one month, you will owe about $55 interest. And that interest gets added to the total amount you owe, so next month, you'll be charged interest on your interest—and it snowballs.

Minimum Payments

Your credit card will require you to make a minimum payment—typically 2 to 3 percent of your balance—every month. If you don't pay the minimum payment on time, you will incur late penalties, typically up to $25 on the first late payment (the late payment will also appear on your credit report). It's important to remember that *paying the minimum payment does not stop the interest from accruing.*

DISCUSS BEFORE YOU GO

- Do your parents want you to use your own credit card for emergencies, or theirs?
- If you use your credit card in an emergency and your family is going to pay you back, how will you make sure the money is in your account so you can pay the balance on time?

STUDENT LOANS

FAST FACT

In 2018, the average monthly student loan payment for borrowers under thirty years old was $351.[vii]

The interest on student loans is typically much lower than on credit cards, and federal student loans have the lowest interest. You must complete a FAFSA to qualify for one of these loans. Some of these loans, called subsidized loans, do not start to accrue interest until you graduate. Student loans from private (non-government) lenders have higher rates, and the interest usually starts accruing immediately, though in most cases you will not have to pay any of the interest while you're enrolled in school.

Just like with credit cards, the name of the game is keep debt down. In chapter 16, you'll learn ways to reduce your spending (and thus minimize your borrowing). But remember—if you have to borrow, student loans are less expensive than credit cards.

TAXES

Taxes are complicated and become more so as your finances become more complex. In spring, your school most likely offers information sessions about filing your taxes (which are due every year on April 15, or the first weekday after April 15 if it falls on a weekend). In the meantime, here's some information you should know about your taxes.

Grants and Scholarships

As a rule, if a grant or scholarship goes directly to your tuition and school expenses, it doesn't count as income on which you have to pay taxes. However, the amounts disbursed to you that you don't spend on books, tuition, and school housing could be taxed.

Tax Dependents

If you are under twenty-four years old and enrolled in an accredited undergraduate program, and your parents are paying at least 50 percent of your support (grants and scholarships do not count toward this), then your parents can claim you as a dependent on their tax returns. But even if your parents claim you as a dependent, you still have to file a tax return if you work.

Calculating Take-Home Pay

Unless you are being paid in cash (such as cash tips or a babysitting job), your take-home pay will be less than your hourly rate times the hours you worked. Several types of taxes come out of your paychecks, including payroll taxes—which pay for federal retirement benefits—and income taxes—which pay for government services.

Use a take-home pay calculator such as the one at www.adp.com to see how taxes will affect your paycheck.

KNOW BEFORE YOU GO

- Is any part of your grants or scholarships taxable? (Leftover money you don't spend on education will be.)
- Does your family claim you as a dependent on their taxes?

DO BEFORE YOU GO

- Calculate your take-home pay for one week at the job you plan to have this semester.

PROTECTING YOUR IDENTITY

Your personal information—particularly your financial information—is worth money. And like anything that is worth anything, the sad fact is that people are going to try to steal it.

It's important to keep your information private. If you are a US citizen or otherwise authorized to work in this country, your Social Security number (SSN) is the Holy Grail of financial information. Treat it like your toothbrush or your smartphone—don't share it.

Here are some of the steps you can take to keep safe:

- Avoid "phishing" scams:
  - If you receive a phone call from someone claiming to represent your bank or credit card company, do not provide your personal financial information, particularly your SSN, to them. Hang up

and call the bank or credit card company's customer service line or chat through their website.

- Do not provide your SSN or login information in response to an email that claims to be from your lender or bank. Again, if you receive an email, contact the company yourself directly by phone or through their website, not through any link provided in the email.

■ Prevent stolen mail:

- Thieves sometimes take credit card offers out of the mail or find them by going through your garbage, apply for cards, and steal the cards when they come. Opt out of unsolicited credit card offers by visiting www.optoutprescreen.com, which will prevent the credit bureaus from selling your information to lenders and those lenders from sending you credit card offers by mail. You should also destroy any mail you receive that lists your name, address, or other personal information. Your school library, mailroom, or safety office might have a shredder available for students. If not, use scissors and make sure to tear up any parts of the letter or offer that include personal information.

■ Stay vigilant:

- Check all your accounts regularly.
- Keep track of your credit and debit cards and cancel them immediately if they are lost or stolen.
- Review your credit report at least once per year (see page 200) and after any incident such as a lost or stolen card.

■ Practice safe online shopping:

- Don't use your credit or debit cards to shop online in public (such as at a café), where people can see the numbers on your screen and photograph them.
- Don't make purchases when you are on an unsecured Wi-Fi connection.
- Don't save payment information on accounts to which someone else might have access.

RESOURCES FOR CONSUMERS AND BORROWERS

Finances can be challenging, but you're not alone. In addition to campus resources like the financial aid office, you can find help from:

- The Consumer Financial Protection Bureau (CFPB), a federal agency that ensures that financial companies including banks and other lenders follow the law and treat consumers fairly. CFPB also has financial information, including information about student loans. Visit www.consumerfinance.gov.

- The Internal Revenue Service (IRS), the federal agency that collects taxes, has a page dedicated to students: www.irs.gov /individuals/students.

- States (and the District of Columbia) have consumer protection offices. You can find yours here: https://www.usa.gov/state -consumer.

MAKING SENSE OF IT ALL

We realize that the material in this chapter is challenging. Many adults who have had credit cards for years—and even mortgages—find it difficult to navigate their finances and make good decisions about credit, banking, and borrowing. By reading this chapter, you've taken a step toward managing your finances and protecting your future. And like all aspects of adulting, protecting your financial health and security involves knowing when to use the resources available to you. At college, this could include your financial aid office, services for first-generation and Pell-eligible students, and financial literacy programs and seminars.

This stuff is important, and it's not always possible to retain a lot of dense information, so as a parting thought, we're going to break it down to the most essential things to remember. We call them:

POINTS SO IMPORTANT WE'RE TELLING YOU IN ALL CAPS LIKE YOUR GRANDPA'S FACEBOOK COMMENTS

Now that we have your attention:

ALL CAPS POINT #1: BORROWING MONEY COSTS MONEY. Pay for *everything* on time and in full.

ALL CAPS POINT #2: TRUST NO ONE. Keep records of everything and keep your financial information secure and private.

ALL CAPS POINT #3: KEEP IT SIMPLE. Everyone makes mistakes, and financial mistakes are costly. Keep it simple by limiting the number of accounts you have, using direct deposit and automatic payments, and taking advantage of apps and organizers.

Now that you've got an idea of how your finances work and how to use credit, it's time to think about spending it wisely and keeping track of it. In chapter 16, we'll introduce you to some rules and tools for budgeting, and you'll get started on your budgeting process.

16

TURNS OUT, THERE'S
A MATH REQUIREMENT:
UNDERSTANDING BUDGETS

If you're making friends with people who want to go out to dinner every night, spending $20 per meal, and you do not have that money to spend, do not do it. I made that mistake and wasted too much money.

—COLLEGE STUDENT

Hey there. We're glad to see you back after chapter 15, which was top-level adulting stuff. Well done. If you had a nightmare about compound interest or overdraft fees, you're in the right place. This is where we'll give you some simple ways to make the most of your resources.

Come to think of it, you did such a great job with chapter 15 that we're going to lower our voices again.

Guidelines for Smart Budgeting:

1. **PLAN THE BIG PICTURE.** Know all your expenses, assets, and expected income for the year, semester, month, week, and day.

2. **DON'T SPEND MONEY YOU DON'T** *already* **HAVE.** Don't count on your tip money or your birthday check until they're safely in your account, and remember to subtract your expected expenses from your bank account balance.

3. **FACE THE MUSIC.** Always know what's coming in, what's going out, and when. Avoiding your financial reality will not make it go away.

4. **SCHEDULE YOUR PAYMENTS.** Make your expenses as regular as possible so you can avoid surprises, late payments, and over-drafts.

5. **SET SYSTEM DEFAULT TO NO AND DEFINE YOUR "UNLESS."** Approach every decision whether to spend money with the assumption that you won't. Use your meal plan; try free activities and food; when you have to spend, get a good deal and spend on something you truly value or truly need.

6. **FEAR OF RUNNING OUT TRUMPS FEAR OF MISSING OUT.** Your opportunities to have a great time in your new community are unlimited. Your resources aren't.

PRO-TIP

Your bank account balance is not the amount of money you have. You have your account balance minus your expected expenses and your credit card balance. Money for your cell phone bill isn't yours; it's the phone company's, even if it's in your account.

ASSESSING AND PLANNING THE BIG PICTURE

When making a budget, you need to think about the timing and frequency of your expenses and income.

As discussed in chapter 15, pay your bills on a schedule. This helps you keep it simple. Knowing when your money will come in and go out will help you plan your payments, determine your disposable income (also known as pocket money, walking around money, and play money), and decide how much money to borrow.

When you're planning your budget, it helps to divide your expenses and income into categories—for example, a laptop purchase is a one-time expense, but you'll pay your cell phone bill every month and will need to budget for that. You might feel pretty rich when your grant money is deposited in your bank account—but remember that that one-time payment has to last, and budget it accordingly. Here are some typical income and expense items for college students, with their frequency:

Incoming Money

- Graduation present—one time

- Grant disbursement—annual

- Internship stipend—monthly (sometimes per semester or summer)

- Paycheck—weekly or biweekly

- Contribution from family—check with them about frequency

Expenses

- Computer purchase—hopefully just once during college

- Student activities fee—annual

- Books—once per semester

- Mobile phone—monthly

- Prescription refills—monthly

- Summer housing rental (if you don't have free housing for the summer)—monthly, for three months

PREPARING TO LIVE ON A BUDGET:
TRACK YOUR SPENDING

Sketching out your financial big picture should give you a sense of how much discretionary money you might have in a month or semester. While you're still at home, you can reality-check your budget by tracking your spending for one week (not while you're on vacation, when your spending habits will likely be different than usual). You can do this any way you want. It's a great opportunity to test drive a budgeting app or your new banking app.

SAVING YOUR MONEY

Default to Free

No matter what it says on your transcript, just about every college student is double-majoring in finding free stuff. From campus events that serve pizza to outdoor movies in public parks, if it's free, college students find it.

FREE PIZZA!

Redeem this coupon for one free slice of pizza at any one of ten student events the first week of school. We know you can find them.

The good news is, there is a lot of free stuff on campus—particularly your first year. You're going to want to hit the town and try new things but remember to first look for free fun. Even if you don't feel strapped for cash, remember that your friends might be in a very different position—and it's unlikely they'll tell you.

> Having to make that first phone call with my parents, begging for money, was very embarrassing. They were very disappointed and couldn't believe I spent all of the money in such a short period of time.
>
> —COLLEGE STUDENT

When You Must Spend, Save

There are some expenses you can't reduce—your student activities fee, for example. Other school expenses are more flexible.

TEXTBOOKS

Textbooks are extremely expensive, and you generally won't need them after the semester is over. Consider buying them used, renting them, using "reserve" copies in the school library, or selling them after the semester ends (unless they will be a useful resource for future classes).

DO BEFORE YOU GO

See if your required course texts are already listed online and calculate their total cost. Look into used copies and rentals. If the books aren't yet listed, mark your calendar to check again at the end of the summer or ask about the books when you email your professors.

MEAL PLANS: NOT ALL SWIPES ARE CREATED EQUAL

College students have an increasingly wide variety of choices for meal plans. In addition to the standard dining hall, which has many all-you-care-to-eat options, choices include on-campus cafés, sandwich shops, and stores. Treat your meal plan like a budget (see chapter 9

Sample Expense Tracking Tool

MONDAY		TUESDAY		WEDNESDAY		THURSDAY	
Purchase	Cost	Purchase	Cost	Purchase	Cost	Purchase	Cost
Daily Total:		Daily Total:		Daily Total:		Daily Total:	

about how to treat your body as kindly as your budget). Get the most value per meal so that you don't end up supplementing your plan out of pocket every day.

WHEN YOU'RE THERE

Some theater companies have student discounts, particularly if you can go to a show at the last minute. Check out local theaters—you might be surprised to find you can see a play for about the cost of a movie and popcorn.

FRIDAY		SATURDAY		SUNDAY		
Purchase	Cost	Purchase	Cost	Purchase	Cost	
Daily Total:		Daily Total:		Daily Total:		Weekly Total:

Having Fun on a Budget

Discovering free stuff is at least half the fun, but here are some leads to get you started:

- Volunteering at concerts or plays gets you in for free. If you're willing to stand and wear an unflattering vest, you can save money and have a great time.

- Public libraries and community centers host concerts, fitness classes, book readings, and movie nights—all for free (sometimes they even throw in the popcorn).

- Outdoor concerts and plays hosted by your city are often free.

- Concerts in churches and other faith communities are often free or donation-optional.

- Always carry your college ID and ask if there is a college student discount.

Your student newspaper is also a great resource for finding free activities around campus.

DO BEFORE YOU GO

- Find your new hometown newspaper's website, which will list events, including free ones. Bookmark the site on your browser and/or download their app on your smartphone.

- Look at the tourism bureau or chamber of commerce website. It will list local attractions, parks, and events such as film festivals and holiday light displays.

Planning to Treat Yourself

If you've ever tried to go on an extreme diet (this isn't healthy—see chapter 9), you probably know it's hard to maintain. Extremes are seldom healthy, and they're usually unsustainable long-term. In college (and in life), you'll find that some things are worth spending on—if you have the money.

Although your default setting should be NO, you will hopefully plan to have some pocket money. This means when deciding whether to spend money, the answer isn't just NO. It's NO, *unless* . . .

Now that you've laid out your expenses and expected income and calculated your monthly discretionary spending, take some time to define your "unless."

- "I won't spend *unless* the club I want to join is doing an activity that costs money, like a movie."

- "I won't spend *unless* I have enough meal swipes to cover the rest of the week and won't need to spend this money on groceries."

- "I won't spend *unless*_____."

Defining your "unless" is a better way of making financial decisions than simply looking at your balance and saying "yes" if there are dollars left.

WHEN YOU'RE THERE

- If you work off campus, pack a healthy lunch rather than eating out (see chapter 9 for food suggestions).

- Limit the number of organizations and activities you're involved in that have membership fees or involve other expenses (see chapter 18).

- Take the lead! Suggest free (seeing a movie on the campus quad) or low-cost (cooking together in the residence hall kitchen) activities. That way you won't have to decide whether to turn down pricier suggestions.

- Pay attention to prices. Often the campus convenience store charges a lot more for necessity items like shampoo than they cost at a grocery store or online.

- Take care of what you have—it's more budget-friendly than replacing things.

Understanding, managing, and budgeting your money is an essential adulting skill that you'll keep using well beyond college. Because most of your food and housing expenses are already covered (see the discussion of the net price of college in chapter 14), the first year of college can be a transitional period between life with family and life out on your own. Regularly revisit the principles you've learned here and, as with all adulting tasks, don't be afraid to seek help and advice from family and college staff and make use of resources offered by banks and communities (see chapter 15).

In the next chapter, you'll learn about involvement beyond the classroom. You'll see that finances can factor into your decisions about activities, organizations, and employment. As you plan your campus and community involvement, remember to think about your budget.

PART VI

LIFE BEYOND THE CLASSROOM

Before I came to college, I'd never lived in a big city before. It was overwhelming at first but also exciting. Now I love to be able to walk or take the metro to almost anything, and I love having every kind of food and experience nearby.

Moving to a campus that's basically in the suburbs was kind of a shock. It was so quiet—and even downtown everything closed so early! I had to get used to the slower pace.

**—TWO STUDENTS IN THE SAME CLASS YEAR
AT THE SAME COLLEGE**

Like in high school, your life in college is about more than classes and the people you live with. In this section, you'll learn how to navigate the new place where you'll spend most of your time: your campus. Then you'll learn about the types of opportunities—social, athletic, spiritual, and career-oriented—you'll find both on campus and off. Finally, you'll find out how to get familiar with and get the most out of the world beyond campus: your new college town.

17

THE LAY OF THE LAND:
YOUR CAMPUS

WHEN YOU'RE THERE

Don't assume that all your classes will be located in the central campus area that you visited on your tour. Many schools—even small ones—have some outlying buildings that take longer to reach. Don't risk being late to your first class by assuming that it meets in the department building; find out where your classes meet at least a day before they start, and find out how long it will take to get to each one.

GETTING SITUATED

You can familiarize yourself with your campus before you even arrive. This will help you in your first week, when you'll have many errands to do all over campus (get your student ID, fill out paperwork for your work-study job, pick up reading packets at the library or copy center, etc.).

FAST FACT

Although the Americans with Disabilities Act (ADA) requires new and newly renovated buildings to be accessible to people with disabilities, some older buildings are exempt. Find out whether there are any buildings on your campus that are not accessible.

DO BEFORE YOU GO
Use a Campus Map to Get Your Bearings

- Find and highlight key buildings: dining hall, wellness center, your residence hall, the library, the fitness center, and the department building for your major (if you have one). *Note:* You might be able to find out where your classes meet before you come to campus. If so, locate those campus buildings. If not, put that on your list of things to do before classes start.

- Orient yourself to north/south/east/west. Is your residence hall west of the main campus green? South of the dining hall? It will be easier to learn your way around if you do this.

- Learn the names of the streets running through and around your campus.

- Use an online map to locate your university within the city, and see where the main roads from campus lead.

- Find out whether there are any spaces on campus that aren't disability accessible. If one of your classes is meeting in a space that is not accessible for you, contact the disability services coordinator, who will ensure that you have access to your class.

CAMPUS TRANSPORTATION

Shuttles

Many campuses have a shuttle bus that runs across the campus and/or to and from public transportation or commercial areas. Don't wait for bad weather or the first time you oversleep to learn the shuttle routes from your residence hall to your classroom buildings.

PRO-TIP

If you attend a summer orientation, take time to practice the routes you'll take once you arrive on campus—for example, from your residence hall to the dining hall or the library. Make a note of how long it takes. Once you move in for your first semester, do a practice walk-through of your routes to classes, too, before they start.

Bicycles

To avoid theft and maintain student safety, many colleges require permits or registrations (usually free) for bicycles. Some will also require you to have safety devices such as reflectors or headlights. Your school's transportation or safety department website will have information about this and other rules and regulations for bicycles on campus—including where you can store them.

Accessible Transportation

Depending upon your campus, there might be additional transportation options for students with disabilities or injuries, including students who travel with an aide. Options might include disability parking permits, on-call accessible vans, and lifts and ramps on shuttle buses.

Your school's disability services office will be able to tell you about accessible transportation options.

Cars and Parking

Many residential colleges and universities don't permit first-year students to have a car on campus, except in special circumstances. If you are considering bringing a car, check with your school first. You might find that your school will not issue you a parking permit.

If you do bring a car, find out your parking options on and off campus. Many schools issue expensive parking tickets for cars without parking permits. Some schools also prohibit students, faculty, and staff from parking in adjacent neighborhoods.

FAST FACT

Your college might have a "good neighbor" policy that prohibits students, faculty, or staff from parking their cars in residential neighborhoods adjacent to campus. If you plan to bring a car to school, don't assume you can use neighborhood street parking unless you are sure it is permitted.

KNOW BEFORE YOU GO

- Does your college require you to register your bike? Will you be required to install reflectors or a headlight?
- What is the best place on campus to meet a ride-share (such as Uber or Lyft) or taxi and are they prohibited anywhere on campus?
- Are there any public transportation stops on or adjacent to your campus?
- When do shuttle buses run, and what is the closest stop to your residence hall and classroom buildings?
- Do you need to show a student ID to ride the campus shuttle?
- Does your campus have a "good neighbor" policy that prohibits you from parking a car on residential streets near school?

CAMPUS RULES AND POLICIES

Policies about guests and the public accessing college facilities vary widely. You will also need to familiarize yourself with your school's policies about access to your campus as a whole and to individual buildings, including residence halls.

Building Access

Many colleges are "open campuses," meaning that the public can enter the campus and most buildings (other than residence halls). Urban college campuses, where school facilities are interspersed with commercial and residential buildings, might have security in building lobbies or require ID card or code access to some buildings.

Find out the open hours for the buildings you will visit most frequently, such as the department office for your major; the library (many are 24/7 but might require you to swipe your ID to enter at night), dining facilities, the health center, and others.

Gender-Inclusive Facilities

A growing number of colleges provide gender-inclusive facilities such as restrooms, locker rooms, and housing. These might include:

- Individual restrooms for use by anyone
- Gender-neutral restrooms in class buildings or residence halls
- Individual locker room facilities
- Policies protecting nonbinary or transgender students' access to the facility appropriate to their gender

- Gender-inclusive housing, where students may select a roommate of any gender

Your college's LGBTQ liaison or student group will have information about gender-inclusive facilities.

Guests

Some college facilities—particularly common spaces—are open to everyone. Others are for university community members and their guests only. If you are planning to have a guest (such as your sibling or a high school friend) visit you, you need to know your school's policies about access to school facilities—particularly residence halls.

General Visiting Policies

Your college most likely has a separate policy about visitors and guests in residence halls—including guests who are students but who do not live in the same building. Here is an example of a residence hall policy at one big-city university:

- Students who live in a residence hall may visit any floor or room provided they follow codes of conduct.

- Students who live in different residence halls may enter any residence hall by swiping their ID at the entrance.

- Students who do not live on campus must present their ID to security before visiting a residence hall.

- Adult non-students must present a government-issued ID, which is kept at the security desk. The host student must meet the non-student at the security desk, escort them to the room or common area, and stay with them for the duration of their visit.

- For longer visits and overnight stays, host students must obtain guest passes for their guests.

Opposite-Sex Visitors

Some schools have specific policies about opposite-sex visitors in residence halls or bedrooms. Your college might limit the hours when opposite-sex guests can be in a single-sex residence hall or in your room; prohibit opposite-sex overnight guests but allow opposite-sex visitors; or maintain different rules for different types of residence halls. For example, one large state university has residence halls that permit opposite-sex visitors 24/7; some with restricted hours daily; and some that do not allow opposite-sex visitors during the week.

Note that even if your school permits visitors, this does not mean that you can let someone move in with you. Your school is likely to have a policy that prohibits visitors from staying for more than three days in a row, limits the total number of overnight visits in any given month, and prohibits visitation that interferes with your roommate's use of your shared room.

KNOW BEFORE YOU GO

- What are the rules for visitors to your residence hall?
- Do you need to obtain guest passes for visitors?

Familiarizing yourself with your campus will give you more confidence getting to orientation activities and when classes begin. In chapter 18, you'll learn about how to get involved both on your campus and beyond.

18

AFTER THE ACTIVITIES FAIR: INVOLVEMENT AND COMMUNITY RESPONSIBILITY

GETTING STARTED ON GETTING INVOLVED

College isn't *only* about absorbing what is taught in the classroom. On campus, learning takes place absolutely everywhere. There's a reason that your involvement in campus clubs and organizations is called *co-curricular* rather than *extra-curricular*—because these activities complement your academic experience. Don't forget that you actually spend most of your time *outside* the classroom in college. Studies show that first-year student involvement in clubs and organizations expands their organizational and managerial skills; grooms them for college-level academic group projects; helps to diversify their friend groups; and prepares them for leadership roles beyond graduation.

Every campus will boast a large number of clubs and organizations that are student-led and usually sponsored by (not run by) a staff or faculty member who is personally or professionally connected to the group's focus. Most often, the clubs and organizations will be gathered under the umbrella of "student activities" or "student involvement"—a group of student affairs professionals who oversee the procedural requirements, meeting and practice space allotment, conduct of student members, and allocation of student activity fees. However, don't think this group is running the show: the students are.

Many new students question the hours they should commit to student group involvement in college, as they are concerned that their new schedule won't allow them enough free time. Some make the mistake of waiting until their second semester to get involved in clubs and organizations, thinking they will explore student groups once they've developed a pattern of homework and studying. *We would argue that this is a pretty serious mistake*—in fact, most first-year students report that they feel *significantly* more connected to their campus and student community if they enmesh themselves in clubs and organizations as soon as possible.

In this chapter, you'll find tips to select and join clubs and organizations on campus, information about the benefits of involvement, and warnings about how to get too overcommitted. We'll also present details on what it means to really be a full-fledged citizen of your new community.

If you've ever wanted to try something new, college is the time to do it. Unlike many high school clubs and activities, with college clubs you can choose your level of involvement. If you don't like something, then you can stop and move on to something else, and you don't have to worry about how it will look on your transcript. On the other hand, a new interest you discover your first year could

Stay the Course, or Try Something New?

People often say that college is a time to reinvent yourself, and in some ways, this is true. You can shed your old high school self (or at least the pieces of it that you want to part ways with) and focus on the areas of your personality and attitude that you'd like to alter. If you were known as the shy kid, you can certainly work on being more outgoing in college. If you were the class clown and always felt the need to be "on," you can take this time to step back and let your serious flag fly. If you were known as a high school actor, drummer, athlete, singer, or debater, for example, you are at a new crossroads and can choose to:

- **REALLY HONE ONE OF THESE PASSIONS AND THE SKILLS NEEDED TO EXCEL IN IT AT THE COLLEGE LEVEL.** Now that your résumé isn't all about gathering various activities, as it may have been in high school, you can really focus on spending quality time on one of these areas. Seek out ways to showcase your talents and put them on your résumé as a transferable skill.

OR . . .

- **DROP ONE (OR ALL) OF THESE IDENTITIES COMPLETELY.** With the exception of some college athletes who must compete in their sport in order to keep their scholarship, your first year of college is an opportunity for you to join some less familiar or unfamiliar activities and try a brand-new identity on for size.

Take my advice when I say, "Leave high school at home." Sure, if you loved Model United Nations in high school you can become involved on campus, but also make sure to branch out and do some exploring. Discover what you are passionate about through attending a variety of club meetings at the beginning of the school year and narrowing the list down to a few clubs you want to join.

Similarly, attend events you typically would not go to. You may form amazing memories in the process.

—COLLEGE STUDENT

Campus Clubs and Organizations

Clubs and organizations play a huge role in student life in college. The two categories are often discussed together, although there are a few differences. **Clubs** are groups of students who gather because they share similar interests, while **organizations** are groups of students acting toward a particular cause. Your college will most likely have an active student club and organizational system that you might have heard about on a campus tour, from an admissions officer, or in printed or online materials. During orientation, students at your school will be encouraged to pursue club and organizational membership opportunities to help them enrich their college experience.

Take advantage of your first year in college and explore your passions through clubs and lectures. You may even decide that the original career path you wanted to take is not right for you.

—COLLEGE STUDENT

To keep it simple, there are really three types of college clubs and organizations:

1. Those that help you
2. Those that help your studies or future career
3. Those that help others

The good news is that often, one student group you join in college may fulfill two or even all three of those categories for you. A hidden benefit of joining a student group as a first-year student is the regular interaction you'll have with upper-class students with similar interests who can offer you advice related to the focus of the group, and also on classes and professors.

There are approximately thirteen thematic categories of clubs and organizations that you'll find at most colleges. Many may look like repeats of those in your high school, but remember, in college they will be completely student-run and usually more narrowly focused. These categories (and some examples) are:

- Academic (Undergraduate History Club or Film Students' Association)
- Cultural Diversity (Cuban Students for Change or Latinx Discussion Group)
- Faith or Spirituality (Hillel or Gospel Choir)
- Honors/Achievement (International Sociology Honors Society or Phi Beta Kappa)
- Sport and Fitness (Intramural Volleyball Team or Hiking Club)
- Political (College Student Republicans or Model United Nations)
- Public Service/Civic (local elementary school tutoring club or Habitat for Humanity)
- Fraternal (social, professional, or community service sorority or fraternity)
- Professional (business club or Future Teachers of America)
- Publications (campus newspaper or photography journal)
- Performance (Shakespeare group or improv comedy troupe)
- Campus Representation (student rep to the board of trustees or campus tour guide)
- Social (Gamers Club or Harry Potter Club)

KNOW BEFORE YOU GO

- Check out the list of clubs and organizations offered on your campus; this should be easy to find through your college's student activities website.
- Make a list of the groups that sound interesting to you, even if you have never been involved with something similar before.
- Remember that you can always start your own club or organization on your campus!

Benefits to Joining Clubs and Organizations on Campus

In addition to becoming acclimated to your campus, when you join a college club or organization, you'll:

- Develop your "people skills," which are important for your future workplace

- Continue to learn how to work with a team (beyond what you did in high school)

- Learn about yourself as a college student as you change and develop

- Have fun, make friends, and take a regular break from your studies

- Engage with diverse groups of people

- Be provided with networking opportunities for future internships and jobs

- Gain managerial skills in a safe environment where some mistakes are expected

- Be able to use the skills you've learned in class in practical situations

- Gain more in-depth leadership skills (beyond those you gained in high school)

- Have opportunities to grow your role from member to officer/ leader over time

- Expand your résumé to show future employers what you accomplished in college

- Connect and build relationships with campus administrators, staff, and faculty

- Enhance the campus community through the creation of educational programs and campus events

How Do You Decide Which Clubs/Organizations to Join, and How Many Is Too Many?

This is a common question first-year college students have, and one that shows an understanding of the college workload. Of course, determining which and how many student clubs and organizations you should join is an individual choice and based on many factors in addition to your class schedule. These include your ability to pay dues and juggle paid work or family commitments.

> It's good to get involved, but getting too involved can be overwhelming and damaging to your educational career. Depending on the activity, it can also be detrimental to your bank account, so keep in mind the price you pay to have a social life. Be involved, but don't get carried away.
>
> —COLLEGE STUDENT

Note that club and organization involvement varies over successive semesters as well. Some students find that the number of groups with which they become involved expands in successive semesters, as they are better able to manage their schedules. Others find that they begin to drop some of their club and organization involvement as they take on internships and paid work in future semesters. Commit to attending the first "welcome" events and membership meetings of the groups you select, and even research the history of the organizations to compare their missions and goals.

We suggest that you sign up for more clubs than you know you can participate in so that you can receive information, attend events, and weed out the ones you don't love to find which you'd like to join. Ideally, we suggest that you find one club or organization with an academic/professional focus, one that offers you time to socialize and relax, and one that provides service to the larger community.

How Accessible Are Clubs and Organizations for Students with Disabilities?

The answer is that they *should be* very accessible. Title III of the Americans with Disabilities Act (ADA) supports the rights of people with disabilities to accessible spaces and other accommodations to help ensure that, among other things, people with disabilities can attend college with a minimum of difficulty and that their right to experience the world of higher education is not infringed upon.

Although student clubs and organizations are not an official university or college office, their activities must be accessible for students (and employees) with disabilities. Students with disabilities must often advocate for their rights by communicating their needs to the leadership of the club or organization. The office of disability services on your campus is a resource that supports both individual students and clubs and organizations.[viii]

Greek Life: To Pledge or Not to Pledge?

About 9 million college students are members of a Greek organization, and joining a sorority or fraternity in college is a huge decision. However, the importance and impact of rushing and pledging varies considerably from one campus to the next. Many families and communities have traditions about involvement in Greek life in college and as alumni. Other families and communities strongly discourage involvement in sororities and fraternities.

Some colleges have a campus social life that revolves almost completely around their Greek system, with up to 80 percent of students participating. Other campuses have a small number of sororities and fraternities that have a moderate impact on the social life of the school. There are other schools that don't have any recognized Greek organizations on campus. In addition, many campuses don't allow their students to pledge a sorority or fraternity until they have completed their first semester or first year of college.

If you are still deciding whether to go Greek, here's a chart to help you weigh your options.

PROS OF RUSHING A SORORITY/PLEDGING A FRATERNITY	CONS OF RUSHING A SORORITY/PLEDGING A FRATERNITY
PHILANTHROPY: Many Greek organizations work hard to instill a culture of service and philanthropy in their members, and many chapters even have leadership positions dedicated to this aspect of Greek life. Some chapters raise thousands of dollars every year, instilling a lasting appreciation for the value of service among members.	**THE PRICE:** Depending upon the organization, the cost of membership can be one of the largest expenses in your college budget, averaging about $1,000 for a single semester at a public university; that amount might cover only local chapter dues, national organization dues, and insurance. There are often additional costs such as clothing and event tickets that are additional costs as well.
NETWORKING: Networking is an integral part of Greek life and provides one of the strongest foundations for social interfacing with peers. Greek organizations are known for helping to build networks of alumni who often prove extremely beneficial to college students and recent graduates looking for internships, employment, or letters of recommendation.	**HAZING:** Many new fraternity and sorority pledges submit to physical, emotional, and psychological manipulation in the name of joining Greek organizations. Although it is technically forbidden on every campus, the reality is that it still happens and is fairly widespread. The majority of hazing on campuses is time-consuming but harmless. However, some is brutal and results in serious injury and even death. *Note: All hazing should be reported.*

(continued)

PROS OF RUSHING A SORORITY/PLEDGING A FRATERNITY (CONTINUED)	CONS OF RUSHING A SORORITY/PLEDGING A FRATERNITY (CONTINUED)
CULTIVATING LEADERSHIP SKILLS: Fraternity and sorority membership helps cultivate leadership skills by participation in the traditions, collaborative activities, and organizational structure of the group. Undergraduate students can actively contribute, coordinate, and lead as brothers and sisters—all valuable skills for a future career.	**ALCOHOL AND DRUG USE:** Alcohol and illegal drugs are part of a common culture in Greek organizations, although a growing number of Greek organizations seek to teach about this culture of abuse and want little part in it. That said, the vast majority of hazing-related deaths have resulted from forced binge drinking, and a large number of campus sexual assault incidents within Greek organizations are connected to alcohol consumption of their membership.
BELONGING TO AN IMMEDIATE "FAMILY": When you go Greek, you will gain a network of loyal friends and a wonderful built-in system of peer support from your sorority or fraternity "family." Friendships in Greek organizations are strongly encouraged between students of different academic standing, offering under-class students opportunities to learn from upper-class peers, who in turn provide leadership and mentoring.	**WEEKLY TIME COMMITMENT:** During rush, nearly all hours outside class are spent in meetings, completing tasks, or simply being present in the chapter house, meeting room, or with the group. These time commitments can have a huge impact on a student's study, sleep, and work schedules, and require excellent time management skills to balance. Additionally, there are often other events where attendance is expected on weeknights.[ix]

What's with All These Different Types of Sports Teams in College?

Your high school probably had both junior varsity and varsity teams, and your town may have offered varied levels of recreational and competitive sports programs. Most college campuses provide students with opportunities of a similar structure. Here are the need-to-know differences so that you are prepared for your first semester:

- **INTERCOLLEGIATE SPORTS** are your school's official varsity teams and compete at the most competitive level. They are sanctioned by the NCAA and organized into divisions and leagues. Many varsity athletes receive financial aid for their participation and juggle a rigorous practice and travel schedule in addition to their status as full-time students.

- **CLUB SPORTS TEAMS** are competitive, play against other (usually local) colleges, require tryouts to join, and provide a coach. Club teams are a great way to continue your experience with organized sports after leaving high school if you will not be competing as a varsity athlete in college.

- **INTRAMURAL SPORTS** are great if you're looking for recreational games. They are the most casual and affordable way to join organized athletics in college. They also offer some of the most diverse sports (including Quidditch and dodgeball on some campuses). These teams benefit people with little free time and don't usually require attendance at every game.

Both club and intramural teams can typically apply for funding from their school or fund-raise for their needs.[x]

BECOMING A RESPONSIBLE MEMBER OF YOUR CAMPUS AND YOUR LARGER COMMUNITY

Becoming an adult means more than just showing up; you should make every effort to become an involved and informed member of both your college campus and larger community. This includes regular attendance at campus events, appreciating the experiences of all students on your campus, casting your vote in campus, local, and national elections, and understanding the community standards set by your college.

Regularly Attending Campus Events

Many first-year students feel overwhelmed by the number of events, lectures, performances, films, and discussion groups advertised regularly on campus in *addition* to the club and organization programming. Some students react by simply shutting down. Of course it is easier to just hang out in your residence hall lounge than to attend an event on campus where the people and even the location are unfamiliar to you.

Our advice is for you to reframe your thinking: these events should be seen as opportunities rather than overprogramming. As we discussed in chapter 3, thinking and learning outside your comfort zone are hallmarks of being a college student. Be open to something totally new and try to attend at least one program per week that sparks your interest (or is completely unfamiliar to you). Students, faculty, and staff on your campus create a multitude of programs each week with a purpose in mind—you. (See chapter 17 for more information about taking advantage of free programming on your campus.)

Understanding Affinity Groups and Why They're Needed

Finding your community on campus isn't always easy, but it is always worth it, especially for students from marginalized communities who may be in an unfamiliar or uncomfortable new environment. Having a group of people who are invested in your personal well-being and academic success is one of the many keys to making it to graduation day in one piece and having a great time along the way.

—COLLEGE STUDENT

An affinity group is a group of people who come together based on areas of common interest, background, and shared experiences. Groups such as the Black Student Association, Korean Student Collective; First-Generation Student Group; Lesbian, Gay, Bisexual, Transgender, and Queer (LGBTQ:) Alliance; Muslim Student Association; and Student Veterans create greatly needed affirming and empowering spaces for students to increase their sense of belonging and combat the isolation that many students experience in college.

The dramatic rise of reported bias incidents and hate crimes on college campuses and in the nation as a whole has increased the need for student dialogue about safety and inclusion. Some schools have only just recently instituted a procedure to report hate crimes on campus and others have yet to do so. This is especially true for students of color at predominantly white institutions (PWIs). In these safe spaces, affinity groups offer the opportunity for in-depth focus on relevant topics in collaboration with others.

> **Adjusting to a new college culture requires finding individuals who, at a base level, can easily understand the cultural and social experiences you bring to campus. Venting to a selected few that you identify with about the feelings of isolation you feel in a classroom when you might be the only one to represent your racial or ethnic community creates a catalyst for building community and adjustment skills.**
>
> **—COLLEGE STUDENT**

Bringing a diverse student body together to form a community is an important goal of many campuses, and affinity groups help students who feel marginalized to meet and form a collective voice. Each group gives members a forum for exchanging knowledge and for problem-solving based on people's real experiences. Affinity groups can break down communication and organizational barriers on campus. They can also help students identify mentors on campus who will help them advocate for their needs. These groups allow for shared experiences in ways that are productive, valuable, and meaningful for the students involved.

For more information on bias incidents and hate crimes, see the

Anti-Defamation League (ADL) at https://www.adl.org or the Southern Poverty Law Center (SPLC) at https://splcenter.org.

Understanding Your School's Conduct Code

Similar to your school's academic integrity code (see chapter 4), your college will have a code of conduct or code of community standards that establishes the guidelines for nonacademic standards on campus and disciplinary procedures for infractions of that code. College conduct codes are designed to respect the varied experiences and needs of their students, faculty, staff, and even visitors to campus.

Some of the items listed in the code will include conduct that threatens or endangers the health or safety of another person, theft and damage to property, alcohol and drug use, possession of weapons, hazing, disruption or obstruction of college activities, unauthorized use of electronic devices, violation of residential life and housing policies, and violation of policies against discrimination, harassment, and sex- and gender-based misconduct. Each college's conduct code will list the sanctions for infractions, such as warnings, fines, restitution, residence hall suspension, transcript notation, expulsion, or dismissal.

Within the framework established in your college's code, individuals are as free as possible to conduct their own decision-making while modeling responsible citizenship. For example, as a student, you have the right to freedom of expression, but you are also expected to exercise concern for the rights of others. You have the right to freedom of discussion, but you are also expected to engage in civil discourse, accepting others' rights to their own opinions. See chapter 1 for more about speech and expression on campus.

KNOW BEFORE YOU GO

Find your school's code of conduct online and read it before you leave for campus so that you are aware of the community standards of your college (and the disciplinary procedures for infractions of that code).

Casting Your Vote: Campus Elections

Campus student government elections are often a young adult's first real exposure to a formalized democratic process when they are finally voting age. It is important that you take the student government elections on your campus seriously and make sure to vote. The student representatives you vote into office can shape the direction of your institution for years to come. If you are passionate about creating change in your campus community, you can also choose to get involved in student government yourself. The officers often have the opportunity to interact with senior level administrators and the board of trustees. Some schools even compensate the student body president for their service to the campus community.

Federal, State, and Local Elections

The US Constitution gives state governments the responsibility to run elections, even for federal offices such as president and US senators. Each state sets the rules for elections, from how to register; when and where people can vote; options for absentee or online voting; and whether you need to bring photo identification to the polls.

FAST FACT

If you attend college out of state, you may vote in your home state or territory, or in the state where you attend college—but *you can only vote in one place.*

Registering: Primaries and General Elections

You must be registered to vote, and in most places you must register before election day. Some states have same-day registration for those who vote in person. Every state has its own rules for registration. See chapter 20 for information on getting involved with the local government of your new college town.

As a registered voter, you can vote in two types of elections for local, state, and federal offices. In *primary* elections, the political parties choose the candidate who will run for office against candidates from the other parties. State political parties set the rules for voting in primaries. In *general* elections, candidates who won their party primaries, along with independent candidates who aren't a member of a party, compete for positions from neighborhood commissioner to president of the United States. It's easy to find your state's or territory's website for voters at https://www.usa.gov/election-office.

Voting by Absentee Ballot

Because college students are often out of state (or across the state from their permanent residence) on election day, many vote by absentee ballot. States' and territories' rules for absentee voting vary widely, and it's important to find out the rules that apply to you before you leave for college.

KNOW BEFORE YOU GO

- When is the next election in the state where you are registered or plan to register?
- What is the deadline to request and mail an absentee ballot if you will be at school on election day?

DO BEFORE YOU GO

- Register to vote!
- If necessary, request an absentee ballot from your home state or territory.

In this chapter, we've introduced the differences between student involvement at the high school level and at the college level. We've explained the ways to get enmeshed in your campus culture outside the classroom quickly and easily to help with your first-year transition. We've also defined what it means to truly become a part of your campus and larger community by understanding the needs of student affinity groups, the standards of conduct expected at your school, and the responsibility of voting.

In chapter 19, we'll turn our attention to the multitude of career center resources and services that will be available to you when you arrive on campus. We will offer tips on which internship- and job-search pitfalls to avoid until you have completed your first semester (or even your first year) of college.

19

WORK IT: CAREER AND
INTERNSHIP RESOURCES

During your first year of college, the career center can appear intimidating and we feel too young to begin using services to find a job, but it's never too soon to start building a network or discovering what your true passion is. The variety of services are built to help students at any point in their education. Career services allow you to network with amazing professionals from your field of interest who provide the top advice and connections to make it easy to turn your goals into a job.

—COLLEGE STUDENT

O ne of your campus's greatest resource is the career center, which provides more services than you can probably imagine. Yet fewer than 20 percent of undergraduate students reach out to their schools' career centers for advice. More frequently, students in the United States use online resources or consult with family members or friends about important career and internship decisions.

You should know that your campus career center offers a host of opportunities to you as you progress through your time in college and your internship and employment needs change.

We strongly suggest that you learn about the resources offered at your college career center by reviewing their website even before you become a first-year student. Then, when the time comes to search for an internship or apply for jobs, you will know where to go and what services are available (and free) to you.

WHEN YOU'RE THERE

Find your campus career center after you have established a routine your first semester, and check out all the resources it offers!

COLLEGE CAREER CENTER SERVICES

FAST FACT

Some individual schools or departments will house their own career centers geared specifically (and sometimes open only) to their students.

Every college or university career center is organized differently, based on the student needs, physical space available, budget, and academic focus of the school. However, most career centers provide a host of online services to their students and alumni. Larger career centers will also offer many, if not all, of these resources in their offices:

- Self-assessments and career-aptitude testing
- Internship (paid and unpaid) search tools
- Job search tools (part-time and full-time, on- and off-campus)
- Networking opportunities
- Résumé, cover letter, and interview preparation
- Databases for job searches and placement

Self-Assessments and Career-Aptitude Testing

You may remember taking a career-assessment test back in elementary or middle school that suggested a future job for you (tight-rope walker, perhaps?). Well, in college, these self-assessments take on a whole new meaning, as your future career is closer than ever before. The process of self-assessment can help you to identify not only future career paths, but can also suggest academic majors that suit your interests, personality traits, and skills.

INTERNSHIP AND JOB SEARCH TOOLS

Your campus career center can help you get ready for all parts of the internship or job search process. Listed on the following pages are the career resources most commonly utilized by undergraduate students when searching for an internship or employment during the school year, for summer break, and after graduation.

Résumés

Career advisers and other career center staff will assist you in creating or updating your professional résumé. They will help you to decide if you will be creating a *chronological résumé* (which lists your education and experience in reverse date order to show employment history and growth) or a *transferable skills résumé* (which highlights skills and experience that are relevant to the employer, rather than chronologically) based on the position to which you are applying. The career center can also provide useful templates and guides for résumé construction.

Cover Letters

The purpose of a cover letter, which should always accompany your résumé when you apply to an internship or job, is to introduce yourself and compel an employer to read your résumé to learn more about you. There are different styles of cover letters, each relevant to different career paths. Your campus career center will guide you on preparing these when the time is right. Note that your cover letter is the first sample of your writing that a potential employer sees, so it deserves time and attention to ensure it makes a good impression.

Writing Samples

Whether you are applying for an internship or job or to graduate schools, you may be asked to provide a writing sample. The goal of a writing sample is to measure your ability to write professionally, clearly, and succinctly. You can certainly write a sample from scratch at the time of your application, but you can also use something you've written previously written.

Mock Interviews

Your college career center may hold mock interviews either in person or by video conference to help calm your nerves before an interview and ensure that your responses to interview questions are concise. You'll receive feedback from a career adviser, and in many cases, you'll be able to see a video of the entire mock interview.

Job and Internship Fairs

At some point during your first year, you will most likely see a job or internship fair advertised at your school or at a neighboring institution. Although these are most often geared toward sophomores, juniors, and seniors, we *strongly suggest* that you drop by and check out the format of it during your first year of college. This way, you'll know what to expect when you attend as a prospective internship or job candidate, and the process won't be quite so overwhelming.

Professional Speakers, Networking Opportunities, and Alumni Connections

Career centers and academic departments will often host guest speakers to talk to students about potential opportunities within industries and career paths. Networking receptions provide the opportunity for students to connect, seek professional advice, and learn more about businesses and organizations. Often, alumni from your school are asked to be part of these events. Definitely make sure to attend some of these programs during your first year of college. Just sit and listen or chat with people in the field and gather information; you will learn a lot.

DO BEFORE YOU GO

Make sure to pack at least one professional or business casual outfit for your first semester of college. You can wear it to a mock interview, to a real interview, to walk around a job fair, or to attend a networking event. It will also be useful if you are invited to meet an important speaker or attend an event as a guest of a faculty or staff member.

If you are unfamiliar with what constitutes *professional* or *business casual* attire, look up the terms!

THE PATH TO INTERNSHIPS

Unless you attend a school that has a mandatory first-year internship or apprenticeship requirement, we strongly suggest that you wait until at least your second semester of college or, better yet, the summer after your first year (or even your *sophomore* or *junior* year of college) to land an internship. Why?

1. Your first year of college should include a period of adjustment to your new schedule: your courses, time for study and homework, co-curricular activities, a social life, and, for many, paid part-time work. Allow yourself this time to successfully transition to campus life.

2. You will be competing for internships and jobs with sophomores, juniors, and seniors who all have greater qualifications than you.

3. As one of the youngest interns on the job, you will most likely be offered an unpaid internship and given more administrative tasks compared to your upper-class student peers.

4. You should focus on performing as well as you can academically. Then you can market that to potential employers.

When the time is right, an internship will enable you to enrich your education with hands-on experiences and to apply lessons learned in the classroom to new professional settings. At that time, you can become familiar with the internship opportunities available to you in your new college town. A few benefits to look forward to and traps to look out for when it's time for you to commit to an internship experience:

- An internship can help affirm your career aspirations and help you develop new skills. It can also help you learn what you *dislike* in a position, organization, or industry. College students report that this information is equally as valuable.

- Internships are about quality, not quantity. You'll hear college students speaking about how many internships they have held. What's more important is the quality of the experiences they have had and the professional connections they have made in the workplace.

- Do your research and don't get trapped in an internship where all you are expected to do is make coffee and file papers. You should expect some internship days to be dedicated to stuffing envelopes, but the *majority* of your work hours should be filled with challenging and meaningful assignments. Asking other students who have interned at the same company or organization is often helpful, and your career center may have useful information to share as well.

- Make sure you know if your school (and your major/minor) accepts or requires academic credit for internships, and if so, how many credit hours will be received by the number of hours you will be working. Some employers require that their interns receive academic credit, but most colleges have a process for awarding credit for internships, and your chosen internship may or may not qualify. Make sure you research your college's process—your academic or career adviser is a good starting point.

- On average, only 40 percent of internships offer hourly wages or stipends. Consider that at some colleges, you must pay to take an internship for academic credit as you would any class. You should weigh the opportunity against your financial need and check if your financial aid package includes internship courses into the semester's costs.

- Don't forget that if you excel in your position and stay connected to the supervisors and other mentors you meet at your internship site, you may walk away with a professional reference or even a job offer down the road. In addition, many surveys show that the vast majority of employers prefer to hire someone who has previously interned somewhere over someone with no prior experience in a workplace.

Working On and Off Campus

BENEFITS OF WORKING ON CAMPUS	CHALLENGES OF WORKING ON CAMPUS
• Your commute will be quick and relatively safe.	• Positions that interest you might only be eligible to work-study students, and you might not qualify (see chapter 14).
• You might have downtime during which you can do homework and read.	• Working, studying, and living at the same location (especially if your campus is small) can begin to feel mundane.
• You can often guarantee regular shifts that can be planned around your class schedule, as your employer understands that you are a student first.	• You might be eligible for work-study, but the positions open might not interest you or might not work with your class schedule.
BENEFITS OF WORKING OFF CAMPUS	**CHALLENGES OF WORKING OFF CAMPUS***
• Companies will probably pay more than on-campus positions for the same work hours.	• Shifts are often irregular or scheduled at the last minute (especially food service or retail).

• The jobs are often more relevant to your career plans than on-campus positions are.	• Commuting costs extra money and takes time from your academic schedule (on top of the time you're actually working at the job).
• These positions give you the opportunity to network with those in a career or field of interest to you.	• Your supervisor regards you as employee, not a student, so they may not be flexible about your need to take time off to study for exams.

*We generally do not recommend that students work off campus during their first semester of college, unless it is financially necessary, because of the extra time commitment involved.

KNOW BEFORE YOU GO

- If you currently work at a chain restaurant or retail store, does your employer have locations in your new town, and if so, would you be able to work there?
- What are the transportation costs to the business and commerce areas near campus, and how long does it take to get there?
- What are the commitments of your class schedule?

VOLUNTEER WORK

Volunteering can be a great way to connect with your new community. As with any work, volunteer jobs can be a strain on your schedule, particularly if you commit to more than ten hours per week or if you have a significant commute. Unlike unpaid internships, many volunteer opportunities involve fewer hours and give you some flexibility.

Volunteer opportunities that can work with a first-semester schedule include:

- Public library programs for children (often just a few hours per week)

- Organizations that serve meals to homeless members of your community (if you are an early riser, you can assist with breakfast before classes)
- A weekly shift at an arts organization such as a museum or historical site
- Volunteering at theater performances or concerts
- Tutoring at an after-school program
- Helping with religious instruction within your faith community

PRO-TIP

You can serve your community while getting access to your city's cultural offerings by volunteering with an arts organization such as a symphony, theater, film society, museum, or ballet company.

Many colleges will offer volunteer recruitment fairs to connect students with local volunteer opportunities early in the semester. These are often run by the career center or by your school's community service or service learning offices. Check out what opportunities are open to you (and yes, all your volunteer work in college should become part of your résumé!).

We've discussed ways in which you can learn about and prepare for the multitude of career and internship resources available at your school. We've also weighed the benefits and challenges of employment on and off campus, internships, and volunteer work for first-year students, and encouraged you to allow yourself the time to transition into your new college schedule before committing to too much. In the next chapter, we'll discuss the final part of college life that you will be exploring beyond the classroom: your new college town.

$$\boxed{20}$$

ACT LOCALLY:
YOUR NEW COLLEGE TOWN

You're not just moving up in the world—you're moving! Going *away* is one of the most exciting things about going to college. It can and should be an adventure, but it can also be a source of stress. After all, you're not just discovering a new hometown—you're leaving your old one behind.

Although the best way to experience your new home is to live there, you can take some simple steps that will make it much easier to settle in and enjoy the place from day one—and avoid the stress of not knowing where anything is or how to get around.

GETTING SITUATED

Depending upon whether you chose an urban campus, small town, or suburban or rural college, your daily life might involve time off campus and in town. In fact, some urban campuses are interspersed with residential and commercial buildings, and you are "off campus" every time you walk out the door of a university building.

It's a good idea to get a sense of your city's size, layout, neighborhoods, landmarks, and relationship to your campus before you go.

GETTING THERE

Your college's website most likely has directions for visitors to campus. If you're flying or taking a train or bus to school, check out how to get to campus in advance and make a plan.

Some college towns are far from local airports, and it's expensive to get to campus. If this is true for you, consider finding a fellow student to share a ride. Your class social media groups are a good place to start—but be safe: verify your fellow rider's identity and status as a student at your school before committing to meet up.

GETTING AROUND

Learning to navigate a new city or town can be intimidating for first-year students—particularly if you are moving from a suburb or rural area to a city, or vice versa. It's worth it, though. Getting familiar with transportation options in advance is a great idea. And once you learn how to get around, you'll be able to enjoy your new home like the locals do.

Public Transportation

PRO-TIP

Some cities, states, and colleges offer free or subsidized public transportation passes to students. Find out whether you are eligible for this benefit and how to get it.

If you head to a city or town for college and you won't have a car, trains and buses will become a key to freedom. Before you go, check out the transit system's website. Many have an online trip planner that lists fares as well. Make note of the lines from campus to points of interest.

Fares and passes for public transportation vary. In the Washington, DC, metro area, for example, you need to purchase a reloadable card to ride the Metro (subway). In New York City, you can pay for individual rides or purchase a 7-day or 30-day pass. Miami-Dade County has a transit discount program for college students.

Accessible Public Transit

Disability-accessible transportation options also vary by city. Some cities have accessible van service that riders can call or reserve on line or through an app. Check the transit system app for disruptions in accessibility, such as elevator outages.

Some transit systems offer reduced fares for riders with disabilities.

KNOW BEFORE YOU GO

- What public transit lines are close to campus?
- What hours do they operate?
- Does your college offer a transportation benefit such as a free or subsidized pass? How do you get it?
- Does your city or state provide students free access or reduced rates? How do you obtain the benefit?
- What accessible transportation options are available and how do you use them?
- To plan your budget and choose a pass option—will classes, co-curricular activities, volunteer work, or jobs require you to take public transit regularly? About how often?

DO BEFORE YOU GO

- If you are planning to fly, and transportation from the airport to campus is very expensive, ask about ride-sharing options with fellow students or your future roommate(s).

- Prepare your smartphone: Download your city's public transportation app, sign up for text alerts about transit delays, and follow the transit system on social media (another way of finding out about delays).
- Put the accessible transportation call line into your contacts.

Ride-Share Services and Taxis

You might need to use taxis and ride-share services. If you have not used them before, here are some basics to keep in mind.

TAXIS

Taxi fares vary widely depending upon the metro area and time of day. Many taxi systems have surcharges for peak traffic hours, and the meter will increase by time instead of distance.

PRO-TIP

In cities with heavy traffic, taxis can take longer than the subway during rush hour.

Some taxi systems accept cash, credit, and debit. A few cities now have taxi apps. Find out before you ride.

A NOTE ON ACCESSIBILITY

Taxis are required by federal law to permit your service animal to ride with you.

TAXI TIPS

Do:

- Stand on the sidewalk.
- Raise your hand high to signal you want a taxi. You can also call, "Taxi!" when a cab approaches you.
- Look at the lighted sign on top of the taxi (in some cities) to see if the taxi is occupied, available, or off-duty.

- Check to see if someone is already waiting for a cab in the spot where you are and if so, pick another spot or wait until they've gotten a cab to hail one for yourself.

- Stand where traffic is heading in the direction you plan to travel (e.g., stand on the northbound side of the street if you are heading north).

Don't:

- Stand in the street.

- Try to flag off-duty or occupied cabs.

- Get ahead of someone else trying to flag a cab.

- Wait in a spot where a taxi can't stop for you.

A NOTE ON UNLICENSED TAXIS

In some cities, especially at airports or train stations, drivers of unmarked cars (those with no taxi sign or ride-share logo) will approach you to offer you a ride for a flat fare. Do not accept a ride from drivers who approach you. At airports, use the taxi line and wait for a marked cab.

RIDE-SHARE SERVICES

Ride-sharing services such as Uber or Lyft are becoming increasingly popular. These services require you to download an app and set up a payment method. If you do not have a credit card, you may still use these services. They accept many kinds of prepaid debit cards.

USING RIDE-SHARE SERVICES SAFELY: It's important to stay alert when using ride-share services. A ride-share vehicle could be almost any kind of car—don't get in the wrong one! Your ride-share app will show you the license plate number and make and model of the car coming to pick you up; compare them before getting in. Also before getting in, ask the driver the name of the person they are picking up. The Uber app has features that let you share information about your trip with trusted contacts so they know where you are. You can also text a photo of your ride-share vehicle to a friend before you leave.

A NOTE ON ACCESSIBILITY

Many ride-share vehicles are not wheelchair accessible. Check the ride-share service websites for accessible options. (As of this writing, Uber had "Uber Wav.")

KNOW BEFORE YOU GO

- How does the ride-share rate compare to cab fare?
- Which ride-share service do you want to use?
- How can you find an accessible ride?

DO BEFORE YOU GO

- Install a ride-share app and set up your payment method.
- If you've never used a ride-share service before, take a practice run before you go to school. This will help you feel more confident the first time you need it when you move.

DISCUSS BEFORE YOU GO

- Ride shares are expensive, but safety (and your family's peace of mind) is usually worth it. Should you use a ride share at night? Will this come out of your overall monthly budget, or will your family pay for this in emergencies?
- If your family is paying for the ride share, will you use their credit or prepaid card or your own?

SAFETY

Make sure you read chapter 11. Some safety practices—such as using familiar walking routes and carrying a whistle—apply whether you are on campus or in town.

GROCERIES

If you are moving out of state, you might be unfamiliar with the local grocery store chains. Look online for the nearest grocery stores to your campus. Read the reviews to find out if they are specialty stores with high prices or traditional stores.

Here's a cautionary tale: A first-year student was not aware that the grocery store closest to campus, a chain that specializes in organic and natural food, cost far more than traditional grocery stores in our city. She quickly ran through her food budget and had to make do without other necessities.

KNOW BEFORE YOU GO

- What are the nearest traditional grocery stores to your campus, and where are they?
- Are there specialty stores of interest to you? (Examples: vegetarian, gluten-free, kosher, halal)
- Does any grocery store near campus offer discounts with your student ID?

TAKING THE TEMPERATURE

If you're moving away, chances are you haven't experienced your new hometown in every season. A student moving from Southern California to New Jersey might be bracing himself for a blast of cold—only to find that the average high temperature in August is in the eighties! That's why if you're moving to a new climate, it's a good idea to check average monthly temperatures and precipitation in your new hometown.

PRO-TIP

If you're moving from a sunny spot to a temperate climate, don't wait until it gets cold to buy a warm coat. Weather can be quite variable in places with distinct seasons. The authors have seen quite a few shivering, disoriented Floridians on our Washington, DC, campus on windy October days.

Don't be afraid to ask classmates for advice about dressing for the weather. Your class social groups can be a great place to ask for recommendations before you shop.

GOVERNMENT

Regardless of whether you decide to vote in the town where you went to high school (see chapter 18 for information about voting), your college town's city and state government still work for you. City and state officials make decisions that affect your life as a student, including:

- Setting prices for transportation
- Passing ordinances about noise (we hear students sometimes have parties) and group houses
- Deciding how many tax dollars to invest for public colleges and universities
- Setting the minimum wage
- Passing antidiscrimination laws
- Maintaining city services

Your members of Congress and senators also make decisions that affect college students, such as funding for student loan programs.

You should know who represents you in local, state, and federal government.

KNOW BEFORE YOU GO

- Who is the mayor of your new city or town? What ward or precinct do you live in? Who is your city council member?
- Who is the governor of your new state? What is the state legislature called? (It could be the general assembly, legislature, or something else.) Who are your state representatives?
- Who are your new state's US senators? In which federal congressional district is your college located, and who is your representative?

PEOPLE

People are what make a community. Even if you are living on campus, the character of your local community will affect and hopefully enrich your life. Restaurants, community festivals, and specialized markets are just some of the things you might discover in your new town.

WORK AND VOLUNTEERING

Whether you decide to read to school kids through your faith community's outreach program or build your career network through an internship, you will find that volunteering and working create ties to your new community.

Learn about jobs and volunteering off campus in chapters 18 and 19.

***

Exploring your new community should be rewarding and fun, but don't feel stressed out if it takes a while to get used to it. No one can be expected to feel like a local in a new town right away. Much like the rest of your transition to college, discovering your community is both exciting and challenging.

You've learned adulting skills such as managing your time and money, staying healthy, and cultivating professional and personal relationships. You've taken some steps to prepare for this transition, such as building your safety kit, going to your medical provider, and compiling important information. And you've had important discussions with family about your expectations, plans, and potential challenges.

You're ready to college.

PART VII

YOUR
TO-DO LIST

1. DO THIS. NOW. SERIOUSLY.

Note: Your school could require other forms. Check your email regularly and submit all forms your school requests.

- ☐ Free Application for Federal Student Aid (FAFSA; page 189)
- ☐ Final high school transcripts
- ☐ Roommate questionnaire and other housing documents (page 139)
- ☐ Housing and meal plan accommodations (page 133)
- ☐ Pre-college doctor's appointment (ideally, you'll arrange this appointment three months before school starts; page 138)
- ☐ Immunization form (and health form, if applicable; page 139)
- ☐ Proof of insurance (or enroll in campus plan; page 150)

2. KNOW AND DO BEFORE YOU GO

Part I: The New College You

Chapter 1: Your Identity: Is Reinventing Yourself a Real Thing?

Chapter 2: Doubling (or Tripling) Down: Sharing Your Living Space

Chapter 3: Beyond Icebreakers: Getting to Know Your College Peers

Part II: College Is School

Chapter 4: What Do You Want From Me? Academic Standards

Chapter 5: Going Pro: Professionalism in College Academics

Chapter 6: Get to the Point: Read and Study with Purpose

Chapter 7: There Are No Bad Writers, Only Unpersuasive Papers: College Writing

- ☐ Consider feedback you've received in high school and set a writing goal for college (page 101)

Chapter 8: Know Your Network: Academic Support

- ☐ Complete an online library tutorial (page 105)
- ☐ Use the library research portal to find an academic journal article (page 105)
- ☐ Find out about tutoring, writing, and other academic support services your school offers (page 106)
- ☐ Find out who your academic adviser is and get their contact information (page 108)
- ☐ Gather your documentation for disability accommodations and begin the process of arranging for them (if applicable; page 110)
- ☐ Contact the student athlete support office to find out the steps you should take (if applicable; page 112)
- ☐ Check your university email daily (page 114)
- ☐ Take an online tutorial for your school's academic portal (page 114)
- ☐ Log onto the course page for each of your courses and check for updates frequently (page 114)
- ☐ Check out academic resources geared to international students and English-language learners (if applicable; page 115)

Part III: Take Care of You
Chapter 9: Eat, Sleep, Pray, Play: Wellness

- ☐ Find out if your residence hall has a kitchen and what cooking implements they have (page 123)
- ☐ Gather recipes from home, including no-cook and microwavable meals (page 123)
- ☐ Check out intramural and club sport opportunities (page 124)
- ☐ Do the 168 exercise (takes one week; page 128)
- ☐ Research religious and spiritual organizations on and off campus (page 133)
- ☐ Learn school's religious accommodations policies and submit requests (if applicable; page 133)
- ☐ Research off-campus support groups (page 136)

Chapter 10: Health 101: Access to Care in School

Chapter 11: You Are Your Own Safety Net: Staying Protected in College

Part IV: The Resident Experts
Chapter 12: Key Players on Campus: Staff and Administrators

- ☐ Learn about your college administrators (page 171)

Chapter 13: Not So Scary After All: Professors

- ☐ Read your professors' bios on the school website (page 184)
- ☐ Program your professors' contact information into your school email contacts (page 184)

Part V: Money Talk
Chapter 14: You're Not a Loan: Paying for College

- ☐ Learn who your assigned financial aid officer is (page 190)
- ☐ Calculate the net price per year of your college education (page 192)
- ☐ Submit required financial aid documents and final high school transcript (page 194)

Chapter 15: Your Life's Transcript: Financial Literacy

- ☐ Take a financial literacy workshop (page 198)
- ☐ Check your credit score and read your full credit report online (page 200)
- ☐ Choose a bank and set up online banking (page 200)
- ☐ Set up direct deposit (page 202)
- ☐ Download your bank and credit card app and practice using them (page 202)
- ☐ Put your monthly banking time in your calendar (page 202)
- ☐ Learn about your student loans (page 201)
- ☐ Learn about your grants and scholarships (page 202)
- ☐ Calculate your take-home pay (if you plan to have a job while in school; page 206)
- ☐ Write down the contact information for your financial institutions (page 208)

Chapter 16: Turns Out, There's a Math Requirement: Understanding Budgets

- ☐ Learn about your expected expenses, resources, and income during your first year (page 213)
- ☐ Select and download a budget app (if not using your bank's budget feature; page 214)

- ☐ Track your spending for one week (page 214)
- ☐ Calculate your textbook costs and see if used books or rentals are available (page 215)
- ☐ Bookmark your college town's newspaper(s)' website and/or download their app (page 218)

Part VI: Life Beyond the Classroom
Chapter 17: The Lay of the Land: Your Campus

- ☐ Download a campus map and print a copy (page 224)
- ☐ Get to know your campus (key buildings, street names, accessibility; page 224)
- ☐ Get to know campus transportation (shuttles, parking, bikes; page 226)
- ☐ Download campus shuttle app (page 227)
- ☐ Register your bike and install reflectors and light, if required (page 227)
- ☐ Learn residence hall rules and policies, including guest policies (page 229)

Chapter 18: After the Activities Fair: Involvement and Community Responsibility

- ☐ Check out the list of clubs and organizations (including affinity groups and Greek life) on your student activities website (page 234)
- ☐ Make a list of activities you might want to be involved in (page 234)
- ☐ Read your school's conduct code (page 243)
- ☐ Learn about election dates, register to vote, and request an absentee ballot, if needed (page 245)

Chapter 19: Work It: Career and Internship Resources

- ☐ Check out your school career center's website (page 248)
- ☐ Take a career-interest self-assessment test (page 249)
- ☐ Reconnect with a teacher or supervisor who can serve as a reference (page 250)
- ☐ Find a writing sample and save it where you can easily access it (page 252)

- [ ] Pack a professional or business casual outfit (page 253)
- [ ] If you might work off campus, research costs and options (page 256)

Chapter 20: Act Locally: Your New College Town

- [ ] Use an online map to become familiar with your college town (page 259)
- [ ] Test your familiarity with your neighborhood (directions, transportation, street names; page 260)
- [ ] Find out about subsidized transportation benefits and how to get them (page 261)
- [ ] Learn about accessible transportation options (page 261)
- [ ] Get your transportation needs in order:
  - Choose a public transportation pass option (page 261)
  - Download your college town's transit app (page 262)
  - Research travel from home to school (page 260)
  - Research taxi options and fares (page 262)
  - Download and set up a rideshare app (page 264)
- [ ] Research grocery store options (discount, specialty, student discounts; page 265)
- [ ] Find out who represents your city and state in government (page 266)
- [ ] Learn about the demographics of your new community (page 267)
- [ ] Learn a few words and phrases in the second most commonly spoken language in your new town (page 268)

3. MAKE YOUR SMARTPHONE SMARTER

Download Apps:
- [ ] Campus safety
- [ ] Campus shuttle
- [ ] Bank and budget
- [ ] Public transportation
- [ ] Health insurance plan

- ☐ Ride share
- ☐ Course portal
- ☐ Electronic documents (such as Google Docs)
- ☐ Local paper

Save Essential Information:
- ☐ Campus map
- ☐ Contact information
    - ☐ Emergency and public safety
    - ☐ Health plan
    - ☐ Health providers
    - ☐ Pharmacy
    - ☐ Academic adviser
    - ☐ Academic support resources
    - ☐ Your new mailing address
    - ☐ Professors
    - ☐ Financial institutions

- ☐ Install college email account.
- ☐ Disable geotagging in social media accounts.

4. BOOST YOUR BROWSER: BOOKMARK THESE SITES

- ☐ Public safety
- ☐ Library
- ☐ Academic advising
- ☐ Local newspaper
- ☐ College newspaper
- ☐ Student loan interest calculator
- ☐ Bank
- ☐ Budget site (if linked to app)
- ☐ Health plan

ACKNOWLEDGMENTS

This book is about adulting. We filled it with advice that we have been sharing with our college students for years but had never compiled in one place nor made available to a wider audience. Our readers will notice a common theme in the book that remains essential through college and beyond: a big part of adulting is seeking and accepting support from others—from experts like health providers to emotional supporters such as friends, family, and affinity groups.

In writing this book, we've done just that: sought advice from experts, diverse perspectives, and helping hands from colleagues. The book is better—and our experience has been far more rewarding—because of the support we received and the people who provided it. In fact, the decision to work as coauthors has made this book so much more than it would have been if either of us had tried to go it alone.

A number of important people helped bring this book to reality. Their contributions were varied: reading draft chapters and providing expertise; offering feedback in focus groups; sharing their experiences and insight as students, faculty, and staff; challenging us to expand the book's scope; encouraging us; helping to spread the word about our project; and even looking after our pets or reminding us to eat and sleep.

For going above and beyond:

Gihan Fernando, Lisa Freeman, Maya Graham, Barbara R. O'Connor, David Reitman, and Marianne Huger Thompson for their collegiality and thoughtful readings of our early drafts;

Our talented editor, Laura Apperson, for her skill and counsel;

Our colleague Chris Moody for helping us share our book with reviewers across the country;

And our friend Allen Cooper, who believed in this project from the start and helped us find a home for it.

Thank you to:

Claudia Ades
Diandra Angiello
Rebecca Archer
Fanta Aw
Leah Baines
Carsen Beckwith
Kayla Black

Paul Bland
Camille Clark
Lisa Colen
Sam Crane
Bette Dickerson
Andrea Felder
Valentina Fernandez

Una Fletcher
Katie Fults
Quintin Gabler
Hope Gelbach
Candace Gingrich
Carly Glazier
Robert Gosselink
Mary Beth Gosselink
Jamie Gottleib
Sara Harberson
James Helms
Natalie Hollis
Rob Hradsky
Lizzie Irlbacher
Olivia Ivey
Maryann Jackson
Emily Kaltreider
Nancy Kaplan
Magdalene Kaur Bedi
Jodi Korb
Jennifer Latino
Katherine Lewis
Jeremy Lowe
Lori Luc
Andrea Malamisura
Alicia Mandac
Sheila McCormick
Jessica McHale
Amanda Nannarone
Kristin O'Keefe

Terra Peckskamp
Kathy Piombo
Ben Railton
Camila Ramirez
Jaydee Reeves
LaFaye Roberts
Astonique Robinson
Bonnie Rubien
Jonathan Santoro
Greg Schaefer
Mark Schaefer
Luke Schleusener
Kristen Schlicker
Jennifer Schwartz
Emilie Shany
Cherie Simpson
Shannon Smith
April Solomon
Izzi Stern
Sheri Stray
Madeline Titus
Devontae Torriente
Aaron Traub
Lindsay Tulloss
Meredith Vaughn
Jessica Waters
Jaris Williams
Robert Wines
Christopher Wood

To our families:

Rick Brenner for your unwavering humor, love, and partnership for thirty-three years and counting.

Talia Brenner and Caleb Brenner for your eyes to the student reader and with adoration and immense pride for being uniquely and wonderfully yourselves. —AMB

Dave Goldberg for believing I could do this.
Jay Schwartz-Stanton, the coolest person I know. An adequate expression of my love and gratitude would greatly embarrass you and fill a whole book. —LHS

NOTES

i. Eric Barker, "This Is the Best Way to Overcome Fear of Missing Out," *Time*, June 7, 2016, http://time.com/4358140/overcome-fomo/.

ii. S. Turkay, "Setting Goals: Who, Why, How?" 2014, https://vpal.harvard.edu /publications/setting-goals-who-why-how.

iii. "U.S. Colleges See a Big Bump in International Students," NPR, https:// www.npr.org/sections/ed/2015/11/18/456353089/u-s-colleges-see-a-big -bump-in-international-students.

iv. Higher Education Research Institute, *The Spiritual Life of College Students: A National Study of College Students' Search for Meaning and Purpose* (Los Angeles: Higher Education Research Institute, 2005).

v. 2016 College Students and Personal Finance Study, https://lendedu.com/blog/college-students-and-personal-finance-study.

vi. University of Connecticut, "Tuition & Fees," http://admissions.uconn.edu/cost-aid/tuition#.

vii. "US Student Loan Debt Statistics for 2018," Student Loan Hero, https://studentloanhero.com/student-loan-debt-statistics/.

viii. "What Are a Public or Private College-University's Responsibilities to Students with Disabilities?," Americans with Disabilities Act National Network, https://adata.org/faq/what-are-public-or-private-college-universitys-responsibilities-students-disabilities.

ix. "Joining a Fraternity or Sorority: The Pros and Cons of Greek Life," *The Quad* (blog), https://thebestschools.org/magazine/joining-a-fraternity-or-sorority-real-pros-and-cons-of-greek-life/.

x. Ben Winck, "Differences Between College, Club and Intramural Sports," Cappex, https://www.cappex.com/hq/articles-and-advice/college-choice/college-life/Differences-between-College-Club-and-Intramural-Sports.

INDEX

Andrea Malkin Brenner, PhD is a college transition educator who speaks frequently with high school students and parents about the challenges related to the transition to college. She draws on her 25 years of experience as a college sociology professor, faculty administrator, and as the designer of American University's first-year experience program. Andrea is the creator of the Talking College™ Card Deck, the original card deck of discussion prompts for college-bound students and their parents. She holds a PhD from American University, an MA from Boston College, and a BA from Brandeis University. See AMBrenner.com for more information.

Lara Hope Schwartz teaches law and government at American University, where she is the founding director of the Project on Civil Discourse. In her teaching and workshops, she draws upon her experience as a legislative lawyer, civil rights advocate, and communications strategist to build inclusive learning communities where robust dialogue thrives. She is a graduate of Harvard Law School and Brown University. See rentlarasbrain.com for more information.